ADB Foreword

As Asia and the Pacific continue on the path of recovery from the global COVID-19 pandemic, it remains imperative that the region's recovery strategies do not undermine achievements to date in reducing dependency on fossil fuels and protecting the environment, for which national and regional infrastructure plans play a key role in economic growth and social development.

Southeast Asia has a major role to play in achieving the Paris Agreement goals and mitigating global warming, but we need to scale up our member countries' ambitious climate projects to meet their Nationally Determined Contributions (NDCs). The region has made significant progress to scale up climate action, and we have witnessed a renewed momentum in the weeks and months up to COP26, but major challenges remain particularly on financing. The Asian Development Bank (ADB) estimates that Southeast Asian countries alone need $210 billion per year, but they currently face an estimated funding gap of over $100 billion per year.

ADB is committed to supporting its developing member countries in tackling climate change. ADB was the first multilateral development bank to set clear climate investment targets for 2030 in its Strategy and has now raised its ambition to deliver $100 billion in cumulative financing between 2019 and 2030 to combat climate change. ADB has recently launched two of the most innovative initiatives for Southeast Asia during the United Nations UN Climate Change Conference of the Parties (COP26) in November 2021 in Glasgow, UK: (i) the ADB Energy Transition Mechanism partnership (ETM), which will leverage a market-based approach to accelerate to accelerate the transition from fossil fuels to clean energy; and (ii) the ASEAN Green Recovery Platform, with total pledges of $665 million managed by ADB to mobilize an additional $7 billion for low-carbon and climate-resilient infrastructure projects in Southeast Asia.

Access to financing remains challenging, as capital shies away from emerging economies. The growing global green bond market has been crucial in generating some of the financing required, but it must expand, and ADB has intensified its efforts since 2020 to grow access to green and sustainable finance through the development of capital markets in the region.

ADB has worked and will keep working with the Government of the Kingdom of Thailand on further developing its capital markets, particularly in support of new green, sustainable, and social issuances. Building on the support provided to the government of Thailand in the issuance of the first sustainable COVID-19 recovery bond in 2020, two additional social and green bonds were issued in Thailand with support from the ASEAN Catalytic Green Finance Facility (ACGF), bringing in an additional THB 5,000 million (approx. $150 million) in funding in 2021.

ADB is proud to support this important and timely report, through technical assistance for the ACGF, as part of a longstanding relationship with the Climate Bonds Initiative in the region. We will continue to work together to grow green finance markets in Thailand and the wider region as we seek to meet our common goals of a prosperous region and a sustainable planet.

Ramesh Subramaniam

Director General
Southeast Asia Regional Department Asian Development Bank

SEC Foreword

The Securities and Exchange Commission, Thailand (SEC) has laid out a roadmap for developing a sustainable finance ecosystem in the capital market which covers six foundation areas: the issuer, the investor, the product, the external reviewer, the information platform, and cooperation.

As a result of the strong collaborative work with local and international partners, remarkable progress has been made on both the demand side and the supply side. The inclusion of 21 Thai listed companies in the Dow Jones Sustainability Indices Emerging Markets indicates that Thai listed companies are increasingly recognised for their environmental, social, and governance (ESG) efforts.[2] Meanwhile, 75 institutional investors with total assets under management of USD326 billion have become signatories to the Investment Governance Code (I Code).[2]

There has also been a very promising trend of sustainable bonds in Thailand. The total value of green, social, sustainability, and sustainability-linked bonds has been growing exponentially, reaching USD8.4 billion (THB262 billion) as of October 2021. In addition, progress has been achieved in creating an enabling environment including the debut of Thailand's first local reviewer TRIS Rating Co., Ltd., and the development of an information platform for the ESG bond.

The SEC firmly believes that the Thai capital market will strive to promote ESG fundraising for green infrastructure investments. Green infrastructure will play a vital role in accelerating the post-coronavirus (COVID-19) pandemic economic recovery while addressing the challenges of climate change. Thus, green infrastructure investment is a promising strategy to achieve the vision of Thailand's new economic model, Bio-Circular-Green Economy (BCG), and to reaffirm its commitment to the United Nations' 2030 Agenda for Sustainable Development and the Paris Agreement.

This Green Infrastructure Investment Opportunities Report (GIIO) features how green or sustainable bonds have been used to finance a range of projects including solar energy plants, wind energy plants, and low carbon transportation. It also elaborates the green investment opportunities in renewable energy, sustainable transport, sustainable water management, and sustainable waste management. It is hoped that GIIO will help address investment opportunities and mobilize capital flow towards green investments in Thailand.

Ruenvadee Suwanmongkol

Secretary-General
The Securities and Exchange Commission, Thailand

PDMO Foreword

The Royal Thai Government (RTG) has been working towards achieving the United Nations (UN) Sustainable Development Goals (SDGs) and has also pledged to slow the temperature rise under the Paris Agreement. In this regard, the RTG has announced plans to promote economic growth that is more sustainable, inclusive and environmentally friendly as stipulated under the Thailand's National Strategy (2018-2037). The RTG has also introduced the Bio-Circular-Green (BCG) Economic Model, which is in line with the UN SDGs, with the objective of turning Thailand into a value-based and innovation-driven economy while at the same time ensures that no one is left behind. Recently, the RTG has also made a commitment to achieve net-zero carbon emission in 2065 and eventually become a carbon neural nation.

Public Debt Management Office (PDMO), as a government agency under the Ministry of Finance, has been actively supporting the RTG in addressing the issues of climate change and social issues. The PDMO has been collaborating with all relevant parties and played a leading role in the initiation of the Sustainability Bond Program and publishing its first Kingdom of Thailand Sustainable Financing Framework (KOT Framework). The KOT Framework is aligned with all relevant international standards, such as International Capital Market Association (ICMA) Sustainability Bond Guideline and ASEAN Capital Markets Forum (ACMF) Sustainability Bond Guideline, and is certified by Sustainalytics.

Thailand's inaugural sustainability bond has been issued in August 2020 with the tenor of 15-years and was very well received from both local and international investors. The proceeds from the bond have been used to support the financing or refinancing of a clean transportation project to help reduce CO2 emissions, i.e. the Mass Rail Transit Orange Line (East), and an employment generation project as part of Covid-19 relief packages. The bond was later listed on Luxemburg Green Stock Exchange (LGX) and received pre and post issuance certification of government sustainability bond (for the MRT Orange Line) from the Climate Bonds Initiative.

Since the inaugural issuance, the PDMO has continuously issued sustainability bond to promote liquidity of the domestic ESG bond market which is critical to providing a strong foundation for green and social investments in the future. As a result, the sustainability bond outstanding size has now reached the committed amount of 147 billion baht (4 billion USD). Furthermore, more than 10 Thai issuers have issued ESG bonds in either local or foreign currency with a total value of more than THB 99 bn (USD 3 bn.).

The PDMO has pledged to provide further support for the development of the ESG bond market and will continue to facilitate the advancing of the green and social developments and investments in Thailand. The PDMO is committed to play our part to contribute to the RTG's efforts in addressing the pressing issues of climate change and mitigating social disparities.

Patricia Mongkhonvanit

Director General
Public Debt Management Office, Thailand

Executive Summary

The Green Infrastructure Investment Opportunity (GIIO) programme aims to identify and demonstrate green infrastructure investment opportunities around the world. It aims to raise awareness of what is green and where to invest and to promote green bond issuance as a tool to finance green infrastructure. To this end, Climate Bonds Initiative (Climate Bonds) has launched a series of country-level GIIO editions to highlight and introduce green infrastructure project pipelines and investment opportunities to both public and private stakeholders, including domestic and international investors, project developers, project owners, and government departments. With the support from the Asian Development Bank (ADB) through its managed ASEAN Catalytic Green Finance Facility (ACGF), the GIIO Report Thailand 2021 was developed by Climate Bonds during June–December 2021, in collaboration with the Securities and Exchange Commission (SEC) and the Public Debt Management Office (PDMO), Ministry of Finance (MoF) of Thailand.

While the Government of Thailand has invested close to THB4 trillion (USD120 billion) in infrastructure in the past decade, the report highlights that Thailand still faces an infrastructure gap and there is room to upgrade its infrastructure quality, with a possible future infrastructure spending gap of up to USD100 billion by 2040 if the current trend of infrastructure investment is not accelerated. The report makes a case that future infrastructure investment should focus on green infrastructure projects, as they present unique opportunities for Thailand to simultaneously recover from the coronavirus disease (COVID-19) pandemic, and to achieve green growth through a transition towards a low-carbon and climate-resilient economy. If leveraged fully, five green growth opportunities—clean energy transition, circular economy models, sustainable urban development and transport models, productive and regenerative agriculture, and healthy and productive oceans—will require USD172 billion in capital investment and can create 30 million jobs in Southeast Asia by 2030. Much of this potential can be captured by Thailand.

This report highlights four key sectors to grow investments in green infrastructure in Thailand: renewable energy, sustainable transport, sustainable water management, and sustainable waste management, and showcases other green investment opportunities in green buildings, smart cities, and coastal management. The report adopts the Climate Bonds Taxonomy to identify potential green infrastructure projects and assets in these sectors. In this regard, the report presents case studies for each key sector. The case studies are part of a sample green project pipeline of 36 projects, which serves to highlight various types of available investment opportunities in the short and medium terms. The report also analyses current green finance developments in Thailand concerning different financing models.

The report argues that Thailand is well positioned to mobilize capital from the capital markets to narrow down the financing gaps in green infrastructure. Thailand has already put in place an enabling policy environment for climate-compatible green infrastructure investment to rapidly scale up, with the promotion of a bio, circular, and green (BCG) economic model compatible with green investments. Thailand has seen promising growth in the sustainable finance market, which provides a timely momentum for boosting green infrastructure investment through green debt instruments. Several ongoing sustainable finance initiatives in the country will enable more uptake of green and sustainable finance in the future. In addition, Thailand has set a net-zero emissions target by 2065 to provide the basis for more ambitious green infrastructure investments for decarbonisation.

Going forward, the report recommends strategic measures to accelerate green infrastructure investment in Thailand, including (i) accelerating the implementation of key measures identified in the Sustainable Finance Initiatives, including the development of a national sustainable finance taxonomy and enhancement of an environmental, social, and governance (ESG) database and information disclosure mechanism; (ii) adopting Global Green Standards–ISO 14000s on climate change and climate and/or green financing; (ii) establishing a green project preparation facility to support the innovative design of green infrastructure projects; (iv) enacting the Climate Change Act (currently under consideration) to drive national climate change actions—including green infrastructure development—in line with global climate change practices that help countries achieve their commitment to the Paris Agreement; and (v) improving the awareness and visibility of green investment opportunities for stakeholders.

Section 1. Green Infrastructure: An Opportunity for Growth

Thailand has been an upper middle-income country since 2011, and has experienced successive decades of remarkable economic growth and social development and made substantial progress towards Sustainable Development Goals (SDGs).[3] The coronavirus disease (COVID-19) pandemic severely impacted the country given its high dependence on trade and tourism, but the economy has shown signs of recovery in the first half of 2021, with expected GDP growth of 0.8% in 2021 and 3.9% in 2022.[4] Additionally, as world leaders pivot towards a green transition to a low-carbon and climate-resilient economy, green infrastructure investment presents key opportunities for Thailand to simultaneously accelerate post-COVID-19 recovery and pursue long-term sustainable growth through low-carbon and climate resilient development.

Thailand is highly vulnerable to the negative impacts of climate change, with floods being the greatest hazard in terms of economic and human impact.[5] A single flood in 2011 caused a total loss and damages cost of THB1.43 trillion (USD46.5 billion), or equivalent to roughly a 1.1% loss in real GDP in 2011.[6, 7] Heavy rainfalls, drought, cyclones, and sea level rise are also major hazards facing the country. Thailand was ranked by the Global Climate Risk Index as the 8th most affected country globally during 1999–2018, and these climate impacts may intensify in future climate scenarios.[8] For example, it is projected that the number of people in Thailand affected by an extreme river flood could grow by over 2 million during 2035–2044, and coastal flooding could affect a further 2.4 million people during 2070–2100.[9]

Thailand intends to reduce greenhouse gas (GHG) emissions by 20%–25% from the business-as-usual level by 2030 as part of its international climate commitment under the Paris Agreement,[10] and has committed to the United Nations Framework Convention on Climate Change (UNFCCC) 2021 Conference of the Parties (COP26) to reach net zero carbon emissions by 2065.[11] The power sector—with electricity production accounting for 36% of total carbon dioxide (CO_2) emissions from fuel combustion—is the largest emitter in Thailand, followed by transport (31%), and industry (20%).[12] In recent years, the country has shifted policy focus towards energy efficiency and clean energy and made promising progress in decreasing energy and CO_2 emission intensity.[13] However, the country still relies heavily on fossil fuels to meet its energy demand and will therefore need to scale up investment in clean energy. Low-carbon investments in other sectors—such as transport, manufacturing, and waste management—are also needed for Thailand to meet its international climate commitment on mitigation.

Apart from climate change, Thailand is facing the challenge of accelerating post-COVID-19 recovery and boosting long-term sustainable economic growth. The economic growth of Thailand slowed during 2009–2019, recording 2.4% growth in the gross domestic product (GDP) in 2019 compared to 5% growth during 1999–2005.[14] Successive waves of the COVID-19 pandemic caused the Thai economy to contract 6.1% in 2020, one of the steepest contractions among the Association of Southeast Asian Nations (ASEAN) countries.[15] To address the COVID-19 crisis, the Government of Thailand launched stimulus spending packages totalling over THB1 trillion (USD30.3 billion). While the public spending helped mitigate the worst impacts from COVID-19 on vulnerable households, economic activity is not expected to return to its pre-pandemic levels until 2022, and the recovery is projected to be slow and uneven.[16]

Green infrastructure has a vital role to play for Thailand to address the twin challenges of post-COVID-19 recovery, and climate change. In the short term, investment in green infrastructure can accelerate the post-COVID-19 economic recovery, while creating new economic opportunities from green jobs and boosting overall national economic competitiveness and green growth. According to the Asian Development Bank (ADB), if leveraged fully, five green growth opportunities (clean energy transition, circular economy models, sustainable urban development and transport models, productive and regenerative agriculture, and healthy and productive oceans) will require USD172 billion in capital investment and could create 30 million jobs in Southeast Asia by 2030.[17] Significant scaling-up of investment in green infrastructure—which is low-carbon and less polluting, as well as climate-resilient—is also key for Thailand to meet its climate commitments and build resilience to the impacts of climate change, as well as to achieve rapid economic development. Green investment opportunities exist in various sectors such as renewable energy, transport, green buildings, water, waste management, smart cities, and coastal protection. These investments will help Thailand better preserve natural assets, decouple

pollutions—including GHG emissions—from economic growth, and strengthen the climate resilience of its infrastructure, economy, and communities to future shocks. As such, green infrastructure investment—and the associated green growth it can deliver—is a promising strategy for the country to meet the economic transformation vision of Thailand 4.0, especially in the context of COVID-19 recovery.[18]

Much investment in infrastructure in Thailand is being carried out through public funding, followed by public–private partnership (PPP) ventures, with PPP becoming a key mechanism used by the Thai government to deliver new infrastructure projects.[19] While the country may experience some delays or short-term re-prioritisation of projects due to the COVID-19 pandemic, the overall infrastructure investment outlook in 2021 and beyond remains positive.[20] However, public funding is not sufficient to meet the growing demand for these new infrastructure investments; new channels will be necessary to mobilize private capital, especially from the domestic financial market which has high liquidity in the system. By developing new infrastructure projects in a "green" manner and using green debt instruments such as green bonds, project developers can mobilize capital from a more diversified base of domestic investors looking for green. This investor diversification effect was evident when the *BTS Group Holdings PCL—the public transport infrastructure company of Thailand—issued a green bond in 2020; the bond was taken up by 33.4% of new investors, including asset managers, banks, insurance companies, cooperatives, and universities.*[21]

Green infrastructure can also position Thailand as an attractive emerging market destination for green investment, thus opening new opportunities for the country to gain preferential access to international green financing. Globally, there is significant demand for green investments. Green debt instruments including green bonds and green loans—with proceeds used for climate-compatible and environmentally sustainable projects—provide useful tools for private investors looking to invest in green assets and projects globally. There is also an increasing demand for sustainable assets from Asian investors. Thailand can take advantage of this demand and attract capital by developing and promoting a green infrastructure pipeline. Going forward, the identification of green infrastructure investment opportunities in multiple sectors can help investors understand that there is a sufficiently large pool of green financially attractive investments in Thailand across several sectors.

From a policy perspective, green infrastructure investment will further accelerate the transition that Thailand has already initiated towards a low-carbon and climate-resilient economy. Thailand has already put in place an enabling policy environment for climate-compatible green infrastructure investment to rapidly scale up. As the overarching development framework, the 20-year National Strategy (2018–2037) of Thailand promotes (i) green growth and sustainable development, (ii) sustainable maritime-based economic growth, and (iii) sustainable climate-friendly based society growth.[22] The Twelfth National Economic and Social Development Plan (2017–2021) has included sustainable development and infrastructure investment as two key national priorities. The Draft Thirteenth Plan (2023–2027)—which is under public consultation as at November 2021—further identifies several strategic priorities which are compatible with a rapid expansion of green infrastructure investment. These include (i) Thailand becoming a global hub of electric vehicles and a multi-modal transport production and logistics hub within the Cambodia, Lao's People's Democratic Republic (PDR), Myanmar, Thailand, and Viet Nam region; (ii) promotion of a low-carbon and circular economy, including through a bio-circular-green (BCG) economic model; (iii) development of smart and sustainable cities; and (iv) climate change adaptation.[23]

Thailand has also seen promising growth in the sustainable finance market, which provides a timely momentum for boosting green infrastructure investment through green debt instruments. The total value of sustainable finance-themed markets in Thailand—including green, social and sustainability (GSS) bonds—stood at USD8.36 billion as of October 2021. With technical assistance from ADB through the ASEAN Catalytic Green Finance Facility (ACGF), the Government of Thailand issued the first ever sovereign sustainability bond (THB30 billion/ USD944.88 million) in ASEAN in 2020,[24] with THB 10 bn (USD 0.33 bn) of the proceeds allocated to finance Bangkok's Mass Rapid Transit Orange East Line[25] and THB 20 bn (USD 0.67bn) of the proceeds allocated to finance a COVID-19 recovery package.[26] The August 2020 bond was re-opened as of November 24, 2020 to secure a further THB20bn (USD 0.67 bn), bringing the outstanding amount to THB50bn (USD1.67bn) at the end of 2020, with the additional THB 20bn (USD 0.67 bn) of proceeds allocated to refinance the expenditures on the expansion of the Mass Rapid Transit Orange East Line[27] The government's sustainability bond framework is aligned with international and ASEAN capital markets standards, and the bond issuance is part of a 15-year, benchmark bond program to be issued in the next two fiscal years in sectors related to green and sustainable infrastructure.[28] The Sustainable Finance Initiatives for Thailand[29] were also launched in 2021, which foresee the

Thai financial sector playing a significant role in financing the transition of the real economy to sustainability, and effectively managing financial risks from ESG issues including climate change.[30] As the Thai green financing market matures, Thailand is well positioned to provide leading deal examples to the Cambodia-Lao PDR-Myanmar-Thailand-Viet Nam region and become a regional hub with expertise in green infrastructure financing.

Thailand Country Facts

Population: **69.9m** (July–2021)[31]

Population growth rate: **0.22%** (May–2021)[32]

Urban population: **51.4%** (2020)[33]

GDP: **USD501.79bn**[34]

GDP growth rate: **0.8%** in 2021 (estimated) and **3.9%** in 2022 (estimated)[35]

Interest rate: **0.50%** (as of June 2021)[36]

Inflation: **3.4%** (April 2021)[37]

Net inflow FDI: **USD4.8bn** (2019)[38]; **-USD4.77bn** (2020)[39]

Government 10 year yield: **1.65%** (May 2021)[40]

Balance of trade: **USD710.8m** (as of March 2021)[41]

Government debt to GDP: **49.64%** (December 2020)[42]

Rating:[43]

Stable (S&P Global Ratings) (April 2020)

Baa1 (Stable) (Moody's Investors Service) (April 2020)

BBB+ (Positive) (Fitch Ratings) (March 2020)

FDI = foreign direct investment

Snapshot: Macroeconomic outlook

Thailand economic growth averaged 8%–9% per year during 1986–1995, making the country one of the fastest growing economies in the world up until the early 1990s.[44] Following a significant GDP contraction from the Asian financial crisis in 1997, the Thai economy rebounded with 5% growth during 1999–2005.[45] The economy then hit a low of 1.0% growth in 2014 before beginning to grow over the following years, reaching 4.2% in 2018[46] then slowing down to 2.4% in 2019.[47] Slower economic growth in the recent decade—along with other development challenges such as income inequality, labour shortages, environmental degradation, and inefficient public administration—presents a key challenge for Thailand to further attain the goal of becoming a high-income country by 2037.[48] Key drivers of slowing growth included weaker demand for Thai exports, slowing public investments,[49] a decrease in the share of private investment to GDP (4% decrease during 2012–2019), low labour productivity growth (only 0.5% in manufacturing and less in services), and inadequate worker skills to modernize manufacturing.[50]

The COVID-19 crisis severely impacted the Thailand economy given its high dependence on tourism, with foreign tourism accounting for 11%–12% of GDP, and tourism-related businesses accounting for 20% of employment.[51] The crisis caused a negative GDP growth of 6.1% in 2020, driven by the decline in private investment (−8.4%), exports of goods and services (−6.6%), and private consumption (−1%).[52] The profound social impacts of the pandemic were reflected by its impact on poverty—which from 2018 to 2019 dropped to 6.2% and increased in 2020 to 8.8%,[53]—on the labour market—with an increase in the unemployment rate of 1.86%,[54]—and on household debt that reached 79.80% of GDP in the fourth quarter of 2020.[55]

With sizable fiscal space before the pandemic, the Government of Thailand responded to the crisis with three successive fiscal packages equivalent to about 10% of GDP.[56] Around 70% of the total package was allocated through cash transfers and subsidies and a smaller share to the recovery of the private sector.[57] Public investment increased by 5.7% in 2020, reflecting the stimulus package spending.[58] The borrowing to finance the COVID-19 stimulus package partly contributed to raising the total public debt level in the fiscal year 2020 to 49.64% of GDP—8.6% higher than in 2019—but remained below the debt ceiling of 60% of GDP.[59] About 92% of the debt is in medium- and long-term instruments and 97% of the debt is denominated in local currency, making debt service in percent of total revenues remain very low and well within the authorities' benchmark.[60] Moody maintained its rating of Thailand at Baa1, with an expectation that Thailand would be able to absorb shock without the long term impact on its potential economic growth.[61]

The economic performance of Thailand over the first half of 2021 showed signs of recovery due to the rebound of global demand and supportive fiscal and monetary policies. In the first half of 2021, Thai exports increased by 15.53%, and imports rose 26.15% year-over-year. The export gains in June 2021—which rose 43.82% from a year earlier—were led by automotive parts, and computers and parts.[62] Seeing the need for additional borrowing of THB1 trillion (USD30.3 billion)[63]—7% of GDP—for more COVID-19-related measures, the Bank of Thailand (BoT) in September 2021 raised the debt ceiling to 70% of GDP from 60% to give flexibility in policy implementation to cope with COVID-19 and support further fiscal economic stimulus.[64] The current monetary policy also aims to accommodate investment for stimulating economic growth in consideration of the COVID-19 pandemic. The BoT set the policy rate of 0.50% per annum in June 2021, which is lower than the average rate of 1.75% per annum.[65] In addition, contributions from financial institutions to the Financial Institutions Development Fund was adjusted from 0.46% to 0.23% of the deposit base to cut off lending rates.[66] Under a flexible inflation targeting framework since 2021, Thailand also targets headline inflation to lie within the range of 1.0%–3.0% for the medium-term horizon and for the year 2021. This is deemed appropriate for addressing the changing inflation dynamics from technological advancements, and the transition into an ageing society.[67]

Given the current outlook, it is projected that the economy of Thailand will grow 0.8% in 2021, and 3.9% in 2022.[68] Factors affecting the growth prospect include vaccination progress, a rebound of international tourism, and the full disbursement of the recently approved THB 500 billion (USD15.19 billion) fiscal response package.[69]

Snapshot: Thailand's infrastructure planning and financing

The Government of Thailand has invested close to THB4 trillion (approximately USD120 billion in 2021 dollars) in infrastructure during 2010–2020.[70] Transport has been the dominant sector in the Infrastructure Development Master Plan (IDMP) 2015–2022, which prioritised the development of the five transport sectors: (i) inter-link railway network, (ii) road networks, (iii) mass transit in Bangkok and neighbouring countries, (iv) enhancement for highway network to link with key areas in the country and with the regional countries in the Greater Mekong Subregion and ASEAN, and (v) water and air transport.[71] The estimated Investment for the IDMP reached THB3.4 trillion (USD100 billion), of which planned spending on major projects on railway and mass transit networks in Bangkok are dominant.[72]

Despite the pandemic, the infrastructure outlook for Thailand remains positive. Infrastructure investment will remain focused on the transport sector and the Eastern Economic Corridor (EEC), according to PricewaterhouseCoopers.[73] The EEC is an area-based development initiative under the Thailand 4.0 economic model, covering three provinces in the eastern region: Chonburi, Rayong, and Chachoengsao.[74] The six EEC flagship projects—which include investment in high-speed rail, airports, and logistic facilities— are implemented under the PPP model, with a total estimated investment value of over THB 600 billion (USD18.2 billion). As of December 2020, public–private partnership agreements for three flagship projects (the Map Ta Phut Industrial Port (Phase 3), the High-Speed Rail Linking 3 Airports (HSR) project, and U-Tapa International Airport) have been signed, with a plan to commence operations between 2024 and 2025.[75]

The Government of Thailand has recently announced the development of the Southern Economic Corridor (SEC), which is strategically designed to complement and optimise the value generated from EEC investments.[76] Under its development framework, SEC aims to build the western gateway for trade and the gateway for the Gulf of Thailand and the Andaman Sea for tourism, establish bio-based and processed agricultural product industries and promote ecological and cultural conservation. The SEC infrastructure— which includes a seaport, bridges, roads, rails, and oil pipelines—will span to the upper southern provinces of Chumphon, Ranong, Surat Thani, and Nakhon Si Thammarat. The first phase of the SEC development started in 2019 and will complete in 2022. The longer term plan from 2023 will consist of 111 projects with an investment of THB102.4 billion (USD3.1 billion). The SEC will merge with the EEC to become a trade and service hub for the Pacific and Indian oceans.[77]

Outside the EEC and SEC, infrastructure investment in Thailand focuses on transport sector projects, especially urban rail systems and inter-city toll roads.[78] The energy sector has seen a slow down in investment due to high system reserve and sluggish electricity demand from COVID-19, but growth in private corporate power purchase agreements (PPA) for renewable energy has been observed.[79]

Public investment dominates infrastructure financing in Thailand, but the emphasis has been shifting towards PPP in recent years. Infrastructure finance in Thailand comes from multiple sources including government budget, state-owned enterprise (SOE) retained income, government and SOE domestic borrowing, sovereign bonds and SOE bonds, PPPs, and the Infrastructure Fund.[80] The key financing sources of the IDMP (2015–2022) are mainly from government and SOE borrowings (52%), while PPPs account for 16%.[81] The Transportation Action Plan 2018 consisted of 44 projects with a total investment budget of THB2,021.3 billion, for which government budget and borrowing together account for 52% of the financing, and PPPs for 24.85%.[82]

Given an expansion in demand for high quality infrastructure, the Government of Thailand has been promoting PPPs as a viable and innovative tool for capital mobilization to meet funding gaps—especially for large-scale projects—and effectively transfer risks by leveraging the private sector financing.[83] Reflecting this emphasis on PPPs, the State Enterprise Policy Office formulated a PPP Strategic Plan 2017–2021, which estimated a total investment cost of THB1.62 trillion (USD48.4 billion) and subsequently developed the PPP Project Delivery Plan 2020–2027, calling for participation from the private sector.[84] The Government of Thailand also issued the Public–Private Partnership Act 2019 (the PPP Act) to promote PPPs as the most effective and preferred alternative to funding infrastructure projects in the country, and stipulates the following eligibility conditions for PPP projects: (i) infrastructure projects in need of private sector funding; (ii) project cost of THB5 billion (USD182 million) at a minimum; (iii) eligible sectors: roads, rail, air, ports or transport by water, water management (irrigation, water works or water treatment), energy, communications, public health,

education, housing, conference centres, and any other projects provided by Royal Decree.[85] Given this public support for PPPs, it is expected that the modality will play an increasingly important role in infrastructure financing—including for climate-aligned green infrastructure—in the coming years.[86] Apart from PPP promotion, the Government of Thailand is also considering an extension in the investment incentive scheme until 2022 to attract more foreign direct investment flows into the EEC zone.[87]

Despite the current infrastructure pipeline and increasing use of PPPs, Thailand still faces an infrastructure gap and there is room to upgrade

its infrastructure quality. According to the Global Infrastructure Hub, Thailand could face a future infrastructure spending gap of up to USD100 billion by 2040 if the current trend of infrastructure investment is not accelerated.[88] When clustered sectorally, infrastructure investment in Thailand needs to come from four major sectors: electricity, transport, telecommunications, and water. Data from the Global Infrastructure Outlook (2017) suggest that the biggest investment gaps lie in all forms of transport-related infrastructure, with the biggest gap in road related investment, followed by ports, and rail. An investment gap also exists in telecommunications (Chart 1).

Chart 1: Infrastructure investment at current trend and investment need by sector in Thailand, 2016–2040

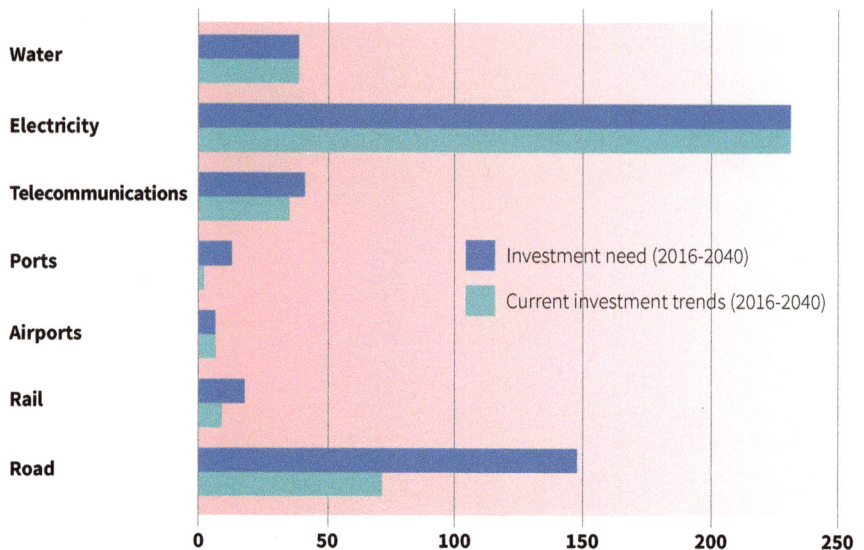

Source: The Global Infrastructure Outlook, 2017[98]

Thailand is increasing climate ambitions both on mitigation and adaptation

Thailand submitted its first Nationally Determined Contribution (NDC) to the United Nations Framework Convention on Climate Change (UNFCCC) in 2016. Under its updated NDC in 2020, Thailand is committed to reducing its GHG emissions by 20% compared to the projected business-as-usual by 2030, using 2005 as the baseline year.[89] This contribution could be increased up to 25% through enhanced access to technology development and transfer, more financial resources, and capacity building support. The updated NDC highlights the need for financial support mechanisms for technical assistance for the energy sector.[90] It also emphasises that Thailand aims to use the opportunity from pandemic recovery to build back better an ecosystem and economy that is climate-resilient and sustainable.[91]

The Thai NDC was formulated based on the Climate Change Master Plan 2015–2050, the Twelfth National Economic and Social Development Plan (2017–2021), and sector plans and roadmaps related to energy, transport, and waste management. Specifically, the Climate Change Master Plan 2015–2050 establishes a national framework for policy development, government action plans, and budgeting on sustainable development, low carbon growth, and climate resilience by 2050. Ambitious energy targets are put forward in the Power Development Plan (PDP), the Alternative Energy Development Plan, and the Energy Efficiency Plan. The Waste Management Roadmap (2018–2030) promotes waste-to-energy technologies, and implements the 3Rs (Reduce, Reuse, Recycle) principles with a focus on circular economy development by recycling 100% of targeted plastic waste by 2027.[92] Thailand is also currently formulating its Long-term Low Greenhouse Gas Emission Development Strategy, which will serve as a basis for enhancing

its subsequent NDCs.[93] The National Energy Plan framework was also approved by the Government of Thailand in August 2021, which sets goals and action plans for achieving net carbon neutrality.[94] Thailand also set the target to achieve carbon neutrality by 2050 and net-zero emissions by 2065, which was announced at the UNFCCC COP26 in November 2021.[95]

Climate policy in Thailand has placed adaptation and mitigation efforts as equally important. According to the National Adaptation Plan, Thailand is focusing its adaptation efforts on key sectors such as energy, water, transportation, agriculture, human settlement, and public health.[96] Adaptation objectives have been integrated into key sector policies and plans, including the Strategy for Climate Change in Agriculture (2017–2021), the Climate Change Adaptation Plan on Public Health (2018–2030), the Water Resource Master Plan, and Spatial Plans.[97]

Section 2. Green Finance Trends and Opportunities

This section presents current trends in green finance and discusses the opportunities that they present for green infrastructure investment in Thailand. It focuses on how Thailand can leverage the green bond markets, other domestic sustainable finance initiatives, and collaboration with international development finance institutions (DFIs) to promote green infrastructure.

Global demand for green is growing

Global demand for green investments is growing with strong momentum and significant growth potential. Green labelled products have become globally recognised as an effective means of directing investment capital towards climate change mitigation and adaptation actions, including through green infrastructure projects. The growing interest from investors in green projects has resulted in the development and growth of innovative financial products including green, social, and sustainability (GSS) bonds and loans, and green indexed products such as sustainability-linked bonds, and sustainability-linked loans.

Green bonds are currently the most developed segment of thematic instruments, carrying greater recognition from the investor base. The COVID-19 outbreak and the need for investments in crisis response and the sustainable recovery it brings have catalysed further growth of the sustainability-themed bonds market beyond the green label; USD700 billion were issued in 2020 within GSS categories, almost doubling from USD358 billion issued in the previous year.[99] ASEAN GSS issuance represented 1.7% of the global total, and 7.6% of all Asia-Pacific issuances in 2020, which represent 23% of global issuances. The total amount of GSS bonds issued globally during 2016–2020 was USD1.48 trillion (Chart 2).

ASEAN is increasingly appealing to investors

The ASEAN sustainable finance market maintains rapid growth despite the negative impact of COVID-19, focusing attention on the need for a sustainable economic recovery.[100] Interest in the ASEAN markets from investors continues to grow (as illustrated in Chart 3). Apart from ASEAN institutions, several foreign entities—including development banks as well as foreign commercial banks—have issued green bonds in local ASEAN currencies, confirming rising demand in regional domestic markets.

Thailand is well-positioned to mobilize capital from the green bond markets to support green infrastructure investment

Within ASEAN, Thailand has a mature bond market. The Thai bond market has grown rapidly in the aftermath of the 1997 economic downturn

Chart 2. Global GSS Debt Markets, 2016–2020

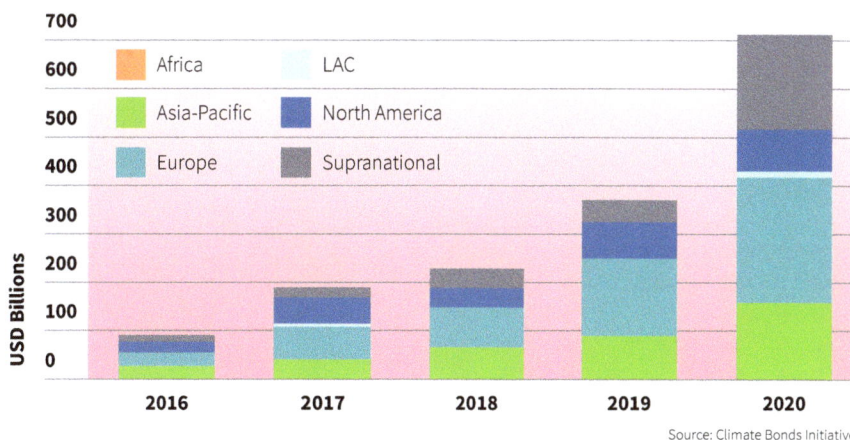

Legend: Africa, Asia-Pacific, Europe, LAC, North America, Supranational

Source: Climate Bonds Initiative

Chart 3. ASEAN GSS Debt, 2016–2020

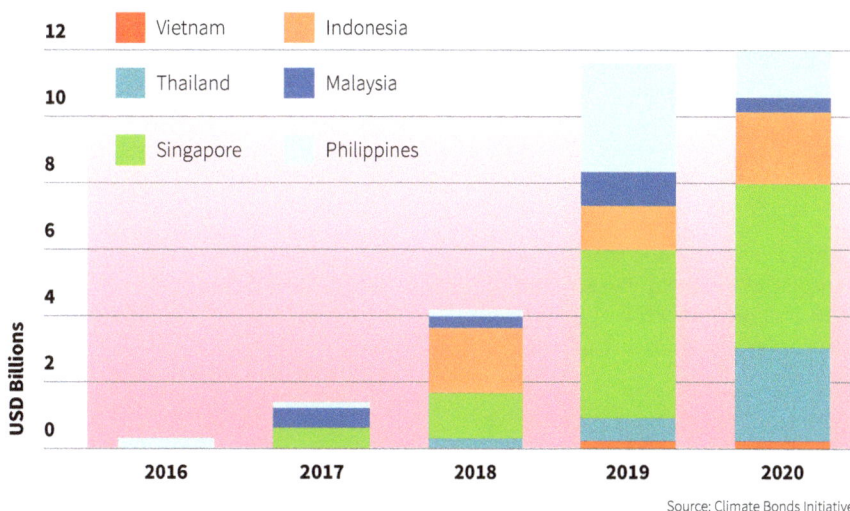

Legend: Vietnam, Thailand, Singapore, Indonesia, Malaysia, Philippines

Source: Climate Bonds Initiative

Chart 4. Outstanding value of the Thai Bond Market, 2010–2020

Legend: Government Bond, Bank of Thailand Bond, Corporate Bond, SOE Bond, Foreign Bond

Source: Thai Bond Market Association[103]

and is the second largest among ASEAN bond markets (next to Malaysia), with an annual average growth of 10%.[101] The Thai bond market has been largely dominated by government bonds—which have seen consistent growth over the years—reaching THB6.02 trillion (USD192.3 billion) in 2020.[102] Corporate bonds remain small compared to the total market value, but the trend has been on the upside in recent years. The outstanding value of the Thai bond market as of 2020 is shown in Chart 4. The existence of a dynamic bond market in Thailand has facilitated the integration of green bonds into the capital structure of the country.

Thailand's green bond market

Thailand began to issue green bonds in 2018, led by private sector issuers.[104] Since then, systems and processes have been put in place to facilitate the growth and to ensure the integrity of green and other thematic bond labels. The Securities Exchange Commission (SEC) issued guidelines on issuance and offer for sale of green, social, and sustainability (GSS) bonds in 2018 and 2019.[105] Issuers are allowed to apply any internationally accepted green, social, or sustainability bond standards, and should also comply with the regulations for conventional corporate bonds. The SEC also encourages GSS bond issuers to appoint an external reviewer and disclose the credentials of the external reviewer and the scope of review publicly on the issuer's website or any designated channel throughout the bond tenure. To incentivise green bond issuance, efforts have been made to offset the additional monitoring and verification costs associated with issuing green bonds. For example, the SEC has introduced waivers for approval and filing fees until May 2022,[106] and the Thai Bond Market Association has reduced bond registration fees.[107] In addition, the SEC has coordinated with international partners (such as ADB and the UK prosperity fund) to support the cost for the external reviewer.

While in a relatively early stage, The Thai green bond market has grown rapidly in recent years. As at 10 November 2021, 22 green bonds were issued in Thailand, totalling USD2.59bn. Apart from the single deal by TMB Bank—which was denominated in USD—all other green issuances were issued in local currency (Table 1). This demonstrates that the Thai bond market is sufficiently mature to support the development of a local green bond market.

Apart from green bonds, Thailand has also seen the growth in issuance of social and sustainability bonds (See Table 2). The total value of the Thai green, social, and sustainability (GSS) bonds market stood at USD8.89bn as of November 11, 2021.

Several institutions in Thailand have successfully issued green bonds to finance green infrastructure investment, particularly for transport and energy

Since the first issuance in 2018, more Thai companies embarking upon a green transition have issued green bonds to finance various types of investments, including green infrastructure.

In 2018, B. Grimm Power Public Company Limited (B. Grimm Power) issued maiden 5-year and 7-year green bonds—the first certified climate bonds issued in Thailand—with proceeds financing renewable energy projects in Thailand.[108] The 2018 TMB Bank issuance was the very first green bond issued by the bank to promote private investments in renewable energy and energy efficiency in Thailand, given that environmental sustainability is one of the pillars of the TMB Bank Sustainable Banking Framework. The proceeds were used to finance climate-smart projects. The International Finance Corporation (IFC) acted as the sole investor of the bond that aimed to provide an alternative source of long-term green finance in the country.[109]

In 2019, Energy Absolute PCL issued its maiden green bond—the first green bond for a wind power project in Thailand—to support the long-term financing of its 260 megawatt (MW) Hanuman wind farm.[110]

Several deals came to the Thai green bond market in 2020. The Global Power Synergy PCL (GPSC), with a THB5 billion (USD153.5 million) green bond issuances for renewable energy and waste projects.[111] The bond was issued in three tranches with 5-, 10-, and 15-year maturities. A Second Party Opinion (SPO) was provided by DNV-GL.[112] The bond received THB30 billion in orders—reflecting a 6-fold oversubscription—which confirms high investor demand for green industry bonds.[113]

Ratch Group Public Company Limited issued a 4 tranche THB8 billion (USD257 million) green bond with maturities ranging from 3 to 15 years. The bond proceeds would be used for investment, repayment, or loans for eligible projects on environmental conservation, consisting of wind power plant projects in Australia, and the Pink Line and Yellow Line electric monorail projects in Thailand.

BTS Group Holdings also issued the largest green bond in 2020 of THB8.6 billion (USD278 million). The deal—which has 5 tranches with terms varying between two and 10 years—would finance and refinance the Pink and Yellow lines of electric monorails in Thailand.[114] BTS Group Holdings is also the first repeat issuer with two deals issued in 2019 and 2020 amounting to THB21.6 billion (USD691.2 million).

Through the Public Debt Management Office (PDMO), the Bank for Agriculture and Agricultural Cooperatives (BAAC) issued its inaugural green bond issuance for THB6 billion (USD180 million), non-guaranteed, through three arrangers— Government Savings Bank, Krung Thai Bank Public Company Limited, and the Hongkong and Shanghai Banking Corporation Limited (Bangkok Branch)—which was offered to Private Placement 10. The bond comprises two series, 5-year green bonds (BAAC258A) of THB4.5bn. with a coupon rate of 1.76% p.a. and a 10-year green bond (BAAC308A) of THB1.5 bn. with a coupon rate of 2.76% per annum.[115] The bond proceeds were used for forestry-related projects.

PTT PCL—a state-owned oil and gas company— issued a green bond for THB2bn (USD65.8 million), with a 3-year term.[116] The proceeds were to finance and refinance investments in environmental projects, such as reforesting various areas of previously forested land throughout Thailand. The project falls under the Conservation and Restoration Forestry segment of the Forestry Criteria of the Climate Bond Standards. The bond was the first of its kind in ASEAN certified under these Criteria.[117]

Among Thai green bonds, energy and transport account for the majority of proceeds allocation. Several green boods were issued by BCPG Public Company Limited to finance renewable energy in 2021 (See Table 1). The remaining spreads across water, waste, land use, and the ICT sectors. The largest issuer in the transport sector is BTS Group Holdings, while the largest in energy is BCPG Public Company Limited. All these issuances (excluding TMB Bank's) obtained external reviews, with nine of them being certified by Climate Bonds.

Thailand has also made use of the sustainability bond label to finance transport infrastructure and post-COVID-19 recovery

Government and development banks globally have been actively issuing bonds to provide immediate relief for the devastating impacts of COVID-19. As echoed by the International Monetary Fund and the Asian Development Bank (ADB), such economic recovery stimulus can accelerate green economic recovery in the greater Asia and Pacific region.[118] Beyond green bonds, there are also social and sustainability bonds, which can be issued to achieve many sustainability goals associated with post-COVID-19 pandemic build back better strategies.

Under the International Capital Market Association Sustainability Bond Guidelines and the ASEAN Capital Markets Forum (ACMF) ASEAN Sustainability Bond Standards, a sustainability bond is defined as a bond where the proceeds are exclusively applied to finance or refinance a combination of both green and social projects that offer environmental and social benefits.[119, 120] Social bonds focus solely on projects and/or assets with social benefits—such as proceeds toward small and medium enterprise (SME) financing and microfinance—or providing access to essential services such as healthcare.[121, 122]

Table 1. Green Bond Issuance, 2018–2021

Issuer name	Amount issued in THB	Amount issued in USD	Issue date	Use of proceeds
SPCG Public Company Limited	THB1.5bn	USD46.87m	Oct-2021	Renewable energy
BCPG Public Company Limited	THB2bn	USD62.5m	Sep-2021	Renewable energy
BCPG Public Company Limited	THB1bn	USD31.25m	Sep-2021	Renewable energy
BCPG Public Company Limited	THB1bn	USD31.25m	Sep-2021	Renewable energy
BCPG Public Company Limited	THB4bn	USD125m	Sep-2021	Renewable energy
BCPG Public Company Limited	THB4bn	USD125m	Sep-2021	Renewable energy
B. Grimm Power Public Company Limited	THB3bn	USD93.75m	Jul-2021	Renewable energy
Toyota Leasing (Thailand) Co., Ltd.	THB2bn	USD64.1m	Apr-2021	Clean transport
BTS Group Holdings (PCL)	THB8.6bn	USD278m	Nov-2020	Transport
Ratch Group PCL	THB8bn	USD257m	Nov-2020	Energy
Global Power Synergy PCL (GPSC)	THB2.5bn	USD80.3m	Aug-2020	Energy, Waste
Global Power Synergy PCL (GPSC)	THB1bn	USD32.1m	Aug-2020	Energy, Waste
Global Power Synergy PCL (GPSC)	THB1.5bn	USD48.1m	Aug-2020	Energy, Waste
Bank for Agriculture and Agricultural Cooperatives (BAAC)	THB 6 bn	USD 187.3m	Aug-2020	Forestry
PTT PCL	THB2bn	USD65.8m	Jul-2020	Land Use
Energy Absolute PCL	THB3bn	USD98.5m	Oct-2019	Energy
Energy Absolute PCL	THB4bn	USD129.5m	Aug-2019	Energy
Energy Absolute PCL	THB3bn	USD97.4m	Jul-2019	Energy
BTS Group Holdings	THB13bn	USD413.2	May-2019	Transport
B. Grimm Power PCL	THB5bn	USD153m	Dec-2018	Energy
TMB Bank	USD60m	USD60m	Jul-2018	Energy, Waste
Total		**USD2.48bn**		

COVID-19 and Other Labelled Bonds

In 2020, Thailand successfully issued an inaugural sovereign sustainability bond via its Public Debt Management Office (PDMO). This is the first sovereign sustainability bond issued in Southeast Asia. The bond—which was issued in taps—totals THB147bn (USD4.76bn) as of November 2021, according to PDMO. The sustainability bond framework is aligned with the International Capital Market Association Guidelines and ASEAN Standards. The bond issuance is part of a 15-year, benchmark bond programme to be issued in the next two fiscal years in sectors related to green and sustainable infrastructure.[123] The use of proceeds has both green and social components: the programme finances green infrastructure through the Mass Rapid Transit Orange (East) Line Project; as well as social impact projects such as public health measures, job creation programmes, and local public infrastructure development to assist with COVID-19 recovery, with related social and environmental benefits.[124] The green tap of the bond was certified against the Low-carbon Transport criteria of the Climate Bonds Standard. ADB supports the Government of Thailand throughout this issuance by providing technical support on bond framework development, external reviews, and the development of systems to monitor the use of bond proceeds and prepare post-issuance reports.[125]

In 2021, ADB also supported the National Housing Authority (NHA) maiden social bond, which was issued on 23 September in 3 tranches totalling THB6.8bn (USD205 million). It is among the first social bonds issued by a state-owned enterprise in Southeast Asia.[126] The bond will finance affordable housing in Thailand and promote sustainable communities.[127] Other green and sustainability bonds are in development.[128]

a. The bond is issued in taps. Initially, the issuer issued THB30 billion but then it reopened the bond and issued another THB35 billion on 21 January 2021. Hence the total amount comes out to be THB65 billion. On 19 March 2021, the government reopened the bond again, making the outstanding amount come out to be THB85 billion (USD3.45 billion) According to PDMO, the outstanding bond value totals THB147bn (USD4.76bn) as of November 2021.

Table 2. Sustainability and Social Bond Issuance in Thailand, 2018–2021

Issuer name	Amount issued in THB	Amount issued in USD	Issue date	Use of proceeds
Thai Foods Group Public Company Limited	THB1bn	USD30.54	Nov-2021	To be determined
National Housing Authority	THB2.1bn	USD62.87m	Sep-2021	To be determined
Kasikornbank	EUR155m	USD182.15m	Aug-2021	To be determined
Bangkok Expressway and Metro Public Company Limited	THB2bn	USD63.81m	Apr-2021	To be determined
Bangkok Expressway and Metro Public Company Limited	THB2bn	USD63.81m	Apr-2021	To be determined
Bangkok Expressway and Metro Public Company Limited	THB1bn	USD31.9m	Apr-2021	To be determined
Bangkok Expressway and Metro Public Company Limited	THB1bn	USD31.9m	Apr-2021	To be determined
National Housing Authority	THB3bn	USD99.22m	Mar-2021	To be determined
National Housing Authority	THB1bn	USD31.91m	Sep-2020	To be determined
National Housing Authority	THB2.8bn	USD89.35m	Sep-2020	To be determined
National Housing Authority	THB3bn	USD95.73m	Sep-2020	To be determined
Bank Of Ayudhya Public Company Limited	USD220m	USD220m	Oct-2019	To be determined
Thailand Government, PDMO	THB147bn	USD4.77bn	Aug-2020	Health care, employment
Kasikornbank	USD100m	USD100m	Oct-2018	Green and social projects
Total		**USD5.88bn**		

Sustainability-linked bonds (SLB)

The issuance of SLBs has also been growing in Thailand. SLBs are any type of bond instrument for which the financial and/or structural characteristics can vary depending on whether the issuer achieves predefined Sustainability/ESG objectives. In other words, the pay-off structure of SLBs is linked to performance targets.

Table 3. Thai Sustainability–linked Bonds, 2021

Issuer name	Amount issued in THD	Amount issued in USD	Issue date
Thai Union Group PCL	THB5bn	USD151m	Jul-2021
Indorama Ventures PCL	THB5bn	USD151m	Nov-2021
Indorama Ventures PCL	THB3bn	USD91m	Nov-2021
Indorama Ventures PCL	THB2bn	USD61m	Nov-2021
Thai Union Group PCL	THB450m	USD14m	Nov-2021
Thai Union Group PCL	THB1.5bn	USD46m	Nov-2021
Total		**USD513m**	

Going forward, Thailand can also consider the use of 'transition bonds' to finance hard-to-abate sectors

The economy of Thailand still depends heavily on the use of fossil fuel resources (Chart 5).[129] Driven by rapid industrialisation and urbanisation,[130] fossil fuel energy consumption in Thailand increased from about 43% of total consumption in 1971 to a peak of 80% in 2014, due mainly to the dependence of industrial and commercial sectors on oil and natural gas.[131] Specifically, more than 60% of electricity production is generated from oil, gas and coal, while on the consumption side, oil-derived energy products and natural gas accounted for around 70% of total final energy consumption in Thailand.[132]

As Thailand is implementing steps to decrease the reliance on fossil fuels and green the economy, **'transition bonds'** can be considered to support this transition from brown to green. The 'transition' concept has been used primarily about high greenhouse gas (GHG) emitting sectors and activities and how to aid their credible transition (Box 1). This recognises that such actors have a more ambitious pathway to transition with significant economic and technological barriers to overcome, but have not played a significant role in the green finance market. The White Paper "Financing Credible Transitions" by the Climate Bonds Initiative—which focuses on transition to net zero by 2050 in line with the 1.5-degree goal—proposes that a **transition label** should also apply to **interim activities**, investments that are making a substantial contribution to halving global emissions by 2030 and reaching net zero by 2050 but do not have a long-term role to play post-2050.[133]

Chart 5. Fossil Fuel Consumption and Electricity Production from oil and gas in Thailand

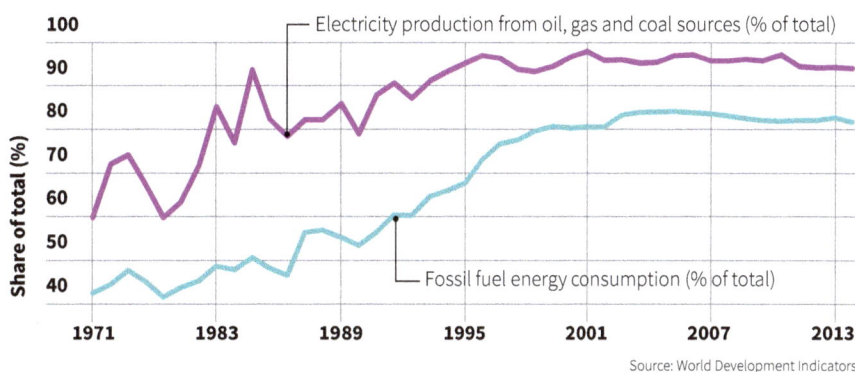

Source: World Development Indicators

Beyond green bonds, Thailand is moving forward with various sustainable finance initiatives which benefit green infrastructure investment

The Government of Thailand has been developing national and regional policies to facilitate further growth in sustainable finance. In 2019, the Thailand Securities Exchange Commission (SEC) approved the Sustainability Development Roadmap to streamline its sustainable finance ecosystem and incorporated it into the SEC Strategic Plan 2020–2022.[134] The roadmap sought to develop sustainable finance in the capital market by developing six main elements: demand, supply, products, and three other enabling factors. In the same year, BoT became a member of the Central Banks and Supervisors Network for Greening the Financial System to enhance the role of financial system to manage climate-related risks.

In January 2021, the SEC became an official supporter of the Taskforce on Climate-related Financial Disclosures.[135,136] In doing so, it takes an important role in c listed companies to adopt international standard disclosure guidelines and incorporate climate-related risks into their strategic planning and risk management. This is expected to enhance the capacity of the Thai capital market for contributing to sustainable development. In 2022, all listed companies will need to disclose the sustainability information integrated with the business reporting called "One-report" as a mandatory requirement, which will include GHG emissions and human rights issues. This illustrates the firm commitment of the capital market of Thailand towards sustainability.

In addition, the Working Group on Sustainable Finance—comprising the Fiscal Policy Office, the BoT, the Thai SEC, the Office of Insurance Commission, and the Stock Exchange of Thailand (SET)—have jointly established the Sustainable Finance Initiatives for Thailand in August 2021.[137] The initiatives recommend five key strategic initiatives, including (i) Developing a Practical Taxonomy (Box 2), (ii) Improving the Data Environment, (iii) Implementing Effective Incentives, (iv) Creating Demand-led

Box 1: Financing Credible Transition

Climate Bonds has been active in promoting the creation of credible transition strategies in GHG-emissions-intensive industries around the world. The concept of transition reflects the fact that in the short to medium term, large companies in many sectors will inevitably straddle both brown and green assets, progressively reducing exposure to brown assets and practices as they increase capex towards—and adoption of—greener modes of operation. It also embodies the recognition that—both globally and locally—institutional investors expect that progress towards low or zero-carbon business models is increasingly indicative of sound corporate performance, hedging of climate risks and long-term value accretion.

Global green investment opportunities are growing and yet large GHG emitters are still largely absent from the market. GHG-intensive segments of the real economy—such as cement and concrete, mining and metals, oil and gas transport, and manufacturing—offer significant emissions reduction potential but are not yet following a transition pathway towards zero carbon by 2050. When such industries start to align with a 1.5-degree emissions trajectory, new green financing opportunities could be created for assets and projects with ambitious climate targets and an increased focus on low carbon production modes.

A credible transition strategy requires organisations to commit to strategic change, undertaking tangible and verifiably climate measures that relate to core business activities of companies. They will need more than broad statements of strategy or intent to disclosure climate risk as envisioned by compliance with the Task Force on Climate related Financial Disclosures.[165] They will need a visible reflection of green investment on balance sheets, in capex plans, and borrowing programmes.

Transition bonds are a highly visible means to support this transition from brown to green. Even a small initial share of green capital expenditure could be a credible indicator of more to come if it is combined with a re-orientation and acknowledgment to investors that achieving low carbon targets and then zero-carbon operating models are inevitable business destinations during 2021–2050, backed up by green spending and capex plans. Transitioning to a green, climate resilient economy is paramount to ensure that the region can reduce its GHG emissions, better hedge against climate change risks, and thrive in the long run.

Box 2: Thailand's Sustainable Finance Taxonomy

A taxonomy is a way of classifying financial flows by assets and/or projects and their relationship to—and impact on—different types of sustainable development. According to the Sustainable Finance Initiatives for Thailand, developing a practical national sustainable finance taxonomy will promote inward investment flows across financial subsectors from domestic and international investors. A well-defined and structured taxonomy also supports better informed and more efficient decision-making and responses to investment opportunities that contribute to achieving national sustainable development objectives. Key recommendations on the next steps for Thailand to develop the taxonomy include:

i. establish a taxonomy working group and undertake stakeholder analysis;

ii. review strategic options (e.g., an overarching versus a more narrowly defined taxonomy);

iii. develop a taxonomy mission and vision;

iv. develop an implementation or project plan; and

v. review results of taxonomy implementation to inform how the taxonomy will evolve.

SEC Thailand also recognises the need to develop a taxonomy that not only addresses local needs but also meets regional ambitions and aligns with international developments. Currently, the Working Group on Sustainable

Finance has initiated a work plan to develop the national green taxonomy to cover the whole financial sector. The working group is currently canvassing technical issues regarding environmental aspects with all related public entities to ensure the applicability of the taxonomy in a local context, and also its alignment with the ASEAN Taxonomy.

Regarding the ASEAN Taxonomy, SEC Thailand has also joined as a member of the taxonomy working group to work on the conceptual framework as the overarching guide to identify and classify sustainable projects and economic activities with inclusivity for the financial sector in ASEAN Member States.

Source: Sustainable Finance Initiatives for Thailand[166]

Products and Services, and (v) Building Human capital. As such, the initiatives will set out the direction and framework for driving sustainable finance across Thailand.

A menu of green financing options in Thailand is expanding

Apart from the green bonds market, Thailand has also been exploring other green finance instruments including equity, credit enhancement and risks mitigation structures (such as partial credit guarantees for green projects), and concessional loans for solar energy and energy efficiency projects (Annexes I through IV provide more information on green financial instruments and mechanisms in Thailand). The expansion of these other green instruments offers promising potential for Thailand to mobilize finance to meet its climate change mitigation and adaptation goals.

Greening the Stock Exchange

Thailand has emerged as a regional leader in ESG disclosure, with 100% of listed companies mandated to report ESG information since 2014.[138] According to the Corporate Knights ranking on the level of sustainability disclosures among companies listed on Stock *Exchange* Sustainability member exchanges since 2012, the SET was the only Asia-Pacific exchange in the top 10 in 2018.[139] In this same year, the SET Thailand Sustainability Index (SETTHSI) was launched to motivate listed firms to adhere their operations to the ESG practices to gain investors' trust and confidence.[140] SETTHSI measures the performance of sustainable companies, which must consider ESG and pass the SET market capital size and liquidity criteria (Figure 1). Since its inception, SETTHSI has performed relatively well, closely following the SET index.[141] According to the Asian Corporate Governance Association and CLSA Securities (Thailand) Ltd, Thai listed companies are among the best in the Asian region in terms of sustainability disclosure.[142]

Figure 1. SET Thailand Sustainability Index (SETTHSI), 2018–2021

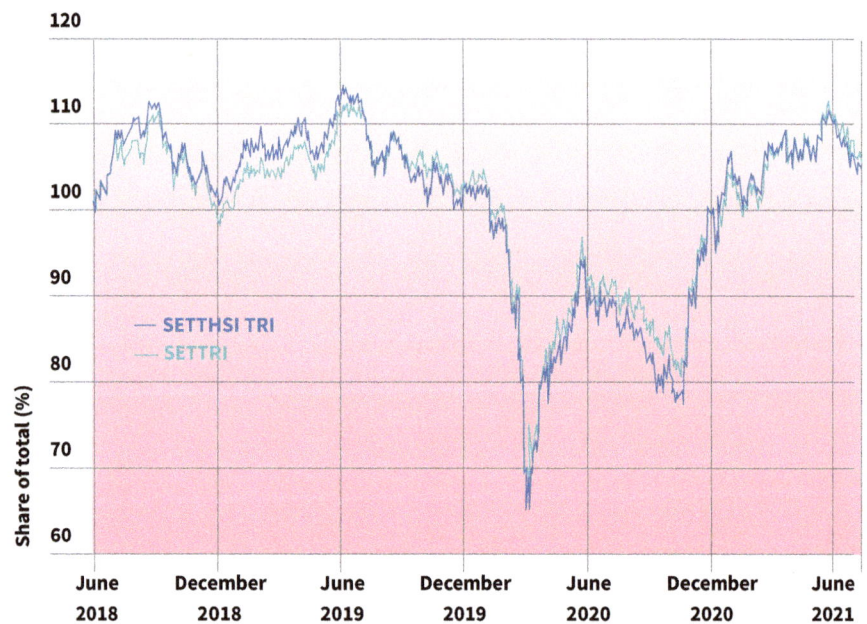

Source: Securities and Exchange Commission of Thailand

The Thai SEC and SET have been providing strategic guidance to issuers on a wide range of topics such as sustainability reporting, sustainability indexing, risks, and materiality.[143] They also encourage large-cap companies to be included in the Dow Jones Sustainability Indices to make Thai listed companies internationally recognised for their sustainable development effort, and attract globally responsible investors.[144] As a result, Thai companies have performed above average in global sustainable indices, with 21 companies included in the Dow Jones Sustainability Indices in 2020.[145]

Thailand has made rapid progress on the quality of its ESG reporting by listed companies. In 2012, the Stock Exchange of Thailand introduced its inaugural Guidelines for Sustainable Reporting

based on the Global Reporting Initiative Framework. Since 2014—under the Thai SEC Sustainability Development Roadmap—Thai listed companies are required to report their policies and activities around corporate social responsibility in their Annual Registration Statement. From 2022 onwards, all listed companies will be required to disclose ESG information rights in the Annual Registration Statement or the Form 56-1 One Report. The disclosure rule includes the integration of ESG issues into business strategies, risks and performance as well as policies and implementation concerning carbon emission and human rights.[146]

In 2017, the Thai SEC published a new Corporate Governance Code which replaced the Principles of Good Corporate Governance for listed companies issued by the Thai SET in 2012.[147] The Code recommends that company boards ensure sustainability reporting using a framework that is appropriate and "proportionate to the company's size and complexity". In response, many companies choose to report their sustainability information against the Global Reporting Initiative framework as per SET guidelines.

Sustainable Banking

Beyond the achievements of the regulators, leadership has been shown in the banking sector. The BoT is ramping up its sustainable finance framework by introducing its 3-year Strategic Plan (2020–2022): Central Bank in a Transformative World.[148] Accordingly, financial institutions are encouraged to integrate ESG information into their business and operating models. The BoT is also a member of the Network for Greening the Financial System and subscribes to its key principles.[149]

In 2019, the Thai Bankers' Association introduced Sustainable Banking Guidelines for Responsible Lending under the leadership of the BoT.[150] Under the guidelines, Thai banks are required to establish internal policies and processes to address key ESG risks in their lending activities.

Private banks in Thailand have led on green finance by issuing green and sustainability bonds to fund and refinance green assets. Thai banks that have issued green and sustainability bonds are TMB Bank and Kasikorn Bank, for USD160 million.[151] Many banks are also providing green loans and other tools for green projects, i.e., renewable energy and energy efficiency. Since 2015, 11 banks have participated in the Energy Efficiency Revolving Fund (EERF), including Bangkok Bank, Bank of Ayudhya, CIMB Thai, TMB Bank, Siam City Bank, Siam Commercial Bank, Kasikorn Bank, Exim Thai Bank, SME Bank, and

UOB.[152] Another example is the "SME Go Green" scheme initiated by Siam Commercial Bank, which provides green loans to green SMEs to cover their long-term and working capital to finance clean energy and pollution management projects which will help to reduce energy consumption.[153]

Green Funds

Thailand has developed several funds for supporting green infrastructure and renewable projects. A domestic initiative is the Energy Conservation Promotion (ENCON) Fund which was established in 1992 under the ENCON Act B.E. 2535 and became operational in 1995.[154] Since its introduction, the ENCON fund is the key financial mechanism of the government to facilitate renewable energy and energy efficiency

development in Thailand. The fund raises about USD200 million each year and had a capital of around USD1bn in 2017. So far, more than 1,000 projects have received capital allocations from the fund.[155] Furthermore, the ENCON fund is also the main funding source for two other successful energy efficiency funding schemes: the Energy Efficiency Revolving Fund (EERF) and the Energy Service Company (ESCO) Revolving Fund. The ENCON fund has resulted in unprecedented success and served as a good reflection of how governments can support the growth of green projects. It is noted that the full methodology for project selection is not available and while it appears broadly aligned with the Climate Bonds Taxonomy and Climate Bonds Standards, there may be some areas where they are not in alignment.

Figure 2. Energy Conversation Promotion Fund

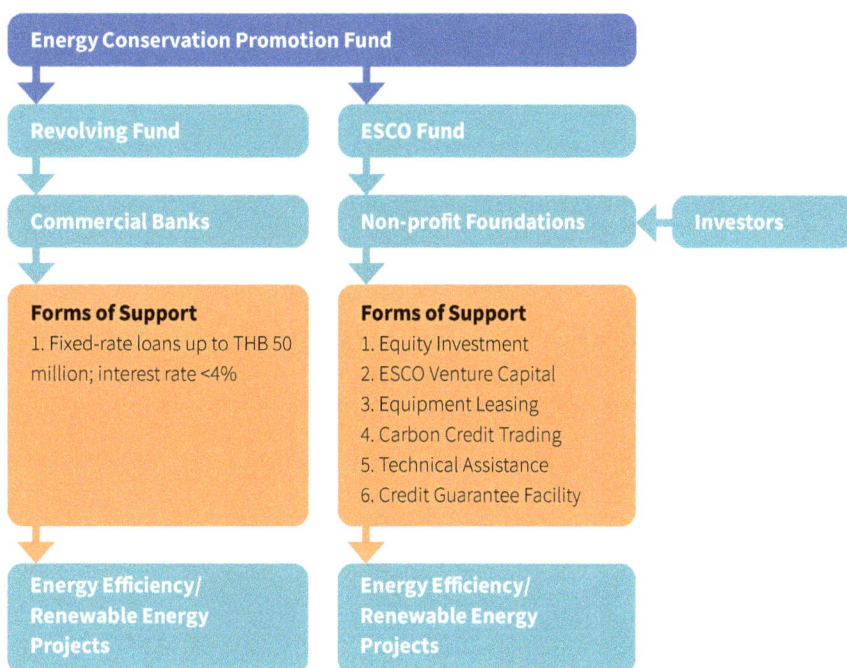

Source: Adapted from Asia-Pacific Economic Cooperation[167]

The Energy Efficiency Revolving Fund (EERF)

The EERF was launched in 2003 to encourage private investment participation in energy efficiency and renewable energy projects and familiarise banks with financing these types of projects.[168] As such, the fund will provide a line of credit to local banks which were then able to lend to project developers with concessional loans. From 2002 to 2019, the EERF was implemented in 7 phases:

Time frame	Phase 1–5	Phase 6–6+
	2003–2013	2015–2019
No. of projects funded	295	160
Total funding provided	THB7.2bn (USD216m)	THB4.2bn (USD126.3m)
Maximum EERF loan size	THB50m (USD1.6m)	THB50m (USD1.5m)
No. of participating banks	11	8
Interest granted to banks p.a.	0.5%	0%
Interest granted by banks p.a.	Less than 4%	3.5%
Electricity energy savings p.a.	1170 MWh	12000 MWh
Total cost savings	**THB6.8bn (USD204m)**	**THB512bn (USD15.4m)**

Table 4. The EERF Timeframe

Thailand is also eligible for some regional and international green funds. At the regional level, the ASEAN Infrastructure Fund Ltd. (AIF)—established in 2011 but formally incorporated in April 2012 and owned by the ASEAN member states and ADB—is dedicated to funding infrastructure development needs by mobilizing regional savings, including foreign exchange reserves. Until December 2020, the AIF has committed an estimated USD500 million for nine projects, with a total portfolio size of around USD3bn, including ADB co-financing.[156] These projects are from Indonesia, the Lao PDR, Myanmar, and Viet Nam.[157] In 2019, the AIF launched the ASEAN Catalytic Green Finance Facility (ACGF) to support governments in Southeast Asia to prepare and finance infrastructure projects that promote environmental sustainability and contribute to climate change goals. In 2021, the AI—through the ACGF—is providing technical assistance support to 29 late stage and early stage projects and concepts (see box on ACGF below).

Thailand can also take advantage of initiatives of international development finance institutions to support green infrastructure investment

The Role of Development Finance Institutions (DFIs)

DFIs have a mandate to support developing countries and can achieve this through blended finance, which refers to the strategic use of development finance for the mobilisation of additional finance towards sustainable development, and credit enhancement mechanisms, both of which reduce risk exposure and enhance market incentives for investors to mobilize private capital.[158] This is particularly relevant for large-scale projects such as infrastructure development, where the blended finance approach can generate more bankable project pipelines by providing technical support and facilitating access to funding.

DFIs that work in ASEAN—such as ADB, the International Finance Corporation (IFC), and the Asian Infrastructure Investment Bank—can subscribe to private placements or be anchor investors in debt issuance and initial public offerings. This will help companies seeking funding to build investor confidence and catalyse investments from a wider pool of private actors. With these interventions, DFIs have leveraged market participation to develop green financing. For example, in early 2019, ADB and other development financiers launched the "ASEAN Catalytic Green Finance Facility" to mobilize USD1bn for financing green infrastructure in

Southeast Asia.[159] In 2 years of activity, the facility has reached USD2bn in pledges to provide loans and technical assistance to sovereign green infrastructure projects in such sectors as sustainable transport, clean energy, and resilient water systems, to promote green and sustainable development in Southeast Asia, and catalyse private capital by mitigating risks through innovative finance structures.[160]

Within Thailand, the IFC has been active in supporting the development of a sustainable finance market. Since 2019, the IFC has joined hands with the BoT to develop a Sustainable Finance Policy Framework, which includes a sustainability roadmap and tools to help banking improve ESG risk management practice.[161]

Likewise, ADB and the Government of Thailand have developed a long-term strategic partnership over the years. Since 1996, ADB has committed USD9.14bn in the forms of loans, equity investment, grants, and technical assistance to Thailand.[162] ADB has been supporting green finance in Thailand by financing or co-financing many green projects in renewable energy, energy efficiency, and sustainable transport. These projects have amplified strategic priorities of ADB to support the Government of Thailand to build inclusive climate and disaster resilience, and achieve its international climate change commitments.[163, 164]

The ASEAN Catalytic Green Finance Facility (ACGF)

Launched in April 2019 under the ASEAN Infrastructure Fund (AIF), the ACGF signifies the commitment of ASEAN member countries to promote sustainable infrastructure development and address climate change in the region. The ACGF supports the ASEAN governments in the forms of loans and technical assistance to identify and prepare commercially viable green infrastructure projects. The ACGF loans are provided by AIF equity finance upfront capital investment costs, while regional technical assistance—administered by ADB and contributed by development partners—assists in project structuring and origination-related activities. This two-pronged approach has made an important contribution to de-risking green infrastructure projects to catalyse investments from private capital investors.[169]

The ACGF provides financing and catalyses co-financing from different partners to support the development of a pipeline of green infrastructure projects in the region, and channels technical assistance support for developing de-risking mechanisms, on a country-by-country basis.[170] For example:

i. Develop de-risking mechanisms such as insurance against specific risks, first loss provisions, purchasing equity, or mezzanine tranches of securitised bonds.

ii. Support for the issuance of tailored structures such as zero-coupon bonds designed to avoid interest during the economic rebuilding from 2021 to 2026, or step-up coupons with a similar objective.

iii. Support for the development of asset-backed structures that would allow for an off-

balance sheet refinancing of sustainable assets and ease pressure on constrained public balance sheets.

These mechanisms could also be available to qualifying bond issuance programmes from commercial banks, municipalities, and private companies.

The ACGF can also support COVID-19 recovery through its ASEAN Green Recovery Platform recently launched at COP26, which will develop and finance green infrastructure projects that align with the ambitions of the Paris Agreement, aspiring to use USD665 million of development funds to catalyse USD7bn for green infrastructure across ASEAN.[171]

Section 3. Green infrastructure investment opportunities in Thailand

This section demonstrates green infrastructure investment opportunities in Thailand and promotes green bonds as an effective financing tool. The section focuses on four major green infrastructure sectors: renewable energy, sustainable transport, sustainable water management, and sustainable waste management. The section also highlights emerging green opportunities from three new sectors: green buildings, smart cities, and coastal zone management.

Methodology

Green infrastructure is low-carbon and less polluting, as well as climate-resilient. The report employs the globally recognised Climate Bonds Taxonomy and Sector Criteria to determine the eligible projects and assets for green investment.[172] The Climate Bonds Taxonomy features eight climate aligned sectors (as specified in the back cover of this report). The Taxonomy aims to encourage common broad 'green' definitions across global markets in a way that supports the growth of a cohesive green bond market. The Climate Bonds Standard and Certification Scheme is used to provide a labelling scheme for bonds and other debt instruments. The Standard and Certification Scheme provides eligibility conditions or thresholds for each type of asset in line with the trajectory toward a 2050 zero-carbon future. The criteria are developed based on climate science by technical expert groups with input from industry.[173]

Based on the methodology, the section considers green investment projects by development status:

i. Completed projects: high profile, recently completed projects;

ii. Projects under construction; and

iii. Planned projects: Major projects that have been announced and/or have undergone business case planning and/or have been allocated budget, but the construction work has yet to start.

Projects selected as case studies include both greenfield and brownfield projects and assets that have been invested and/or are potentially financed or refinanced by green bonds. Based on this, a list of 36 green infrastructure projects is provided as a sample pipeline (Annex VI). Green bonds—as well as other thematic bonds (such as sustainability bonds)—are a promising financing tool to mobilize capital for investment in this pipeline.

What can be labelled green?

Solar and wind. Solar energy—which can be generated using **photovoltaics (PVs–solar cells) and concentrated solar power** (mirrors to concentrate solar rays)—is used worldwide and is increasingly popular for generating electricity or heating and desalinating water.[198] Wind power is one of the fastest growing renewable energy technologies, with usage on the rise worldwide, in part because costs are falling.[199]

More than 80% of all new electricity capacity added in 2020 was renewable, with solar and wind accounting for 91% of new renewables.[200]

Hydropower (some). Hydropower is the largest source of renewable electricity in the world, producing around 17% of the world's electricity from over 1,200 GW of installed capacity. According to the International Energy Agency, hydropower is expected to remain the largest source of renewable electricity generation in the world by 2022.[201] However, it is important to define and adhere to certain thresholds for hydropower development to ensure compatibility with climate change resilience, as well as improvement of environmental and social sustainability. This is important for providing credibility to the market and increasing access to responsible investment options.

Transport (rail and electric urban mobility). 75% of countries have established strategies and targets to improve the environmental performance of their transport sector within their Nationally Determined Contributions (NDCs). One-fifth of the transport-related NDCs include measures in the railway sector.[202]

Sustainable Water Management. The planet is facing a 40% shortfall in water supply by 2030 unless the world dramatically improves the management of this precious resource.[203]

Buildings. Building-related emissions account for about one-third of global GHG emissions and could double by 2050, making building efficiency a critical part of the global climate agenda.[204]

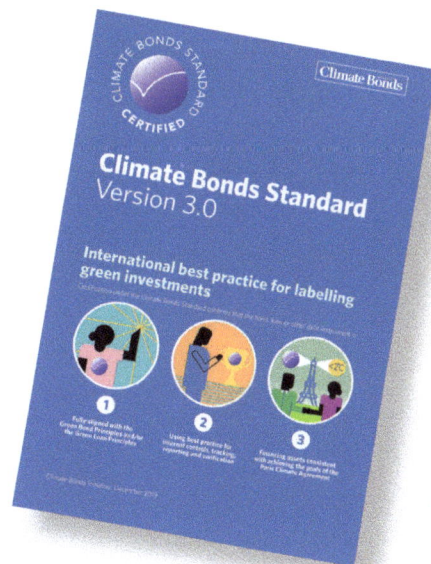

What's green?

Geothermal:

According to the Geothermal Energy Association, 39 countries could supply 100% of their electricity needs from geothermal energy, yet only 6% to 7% of the world's potential geothermal power has been tapped.[205]

Drawdown Agenda

Solar:

The world installed a record number of new solar power projects in 2017, more than net additions of coal, gas and nuclear plants put together.[207]

UNFCCC

Hydropower:

Hydropower is the largest source of renewable electricity in the world, producing around 17% of the world's electricity from over 1 200 GW of installed capacity, and is expected to remain the world's largest source of renewable electricity generation by 2022.[206]

International Energy Agency

© Climate Bonds Initiative

Transport (rail):

75% of the world's countries have established strategies and targets to improve the environmental performance of their transport sector within their Intended Nationally Determined Contributions (INDCs). One-fifth of the transport-related (I)NDCs include measures in the railway sector.[208]

UNFCCC

Water:

The UN says the planet is facing a 40% shortfall in water supply by 2030, unless the world dramatically improves the management of this precious resource.[209]

UNFCCC

Buildings:

Building-related emissions account for about one-third of global GHG emissions and could double by 2050, making building efficiency a critical part of the COP21 agenda.[210]

GreenBiz

Renewable energy

Chart 6. Final energy consumption, 2010–2020

Legend: ■ Petroleum ■ Electricity ■ Natural Gas ■ Coal/Lignite ■ Renewable Energy ■ Final Energy Consumption (KTOE)

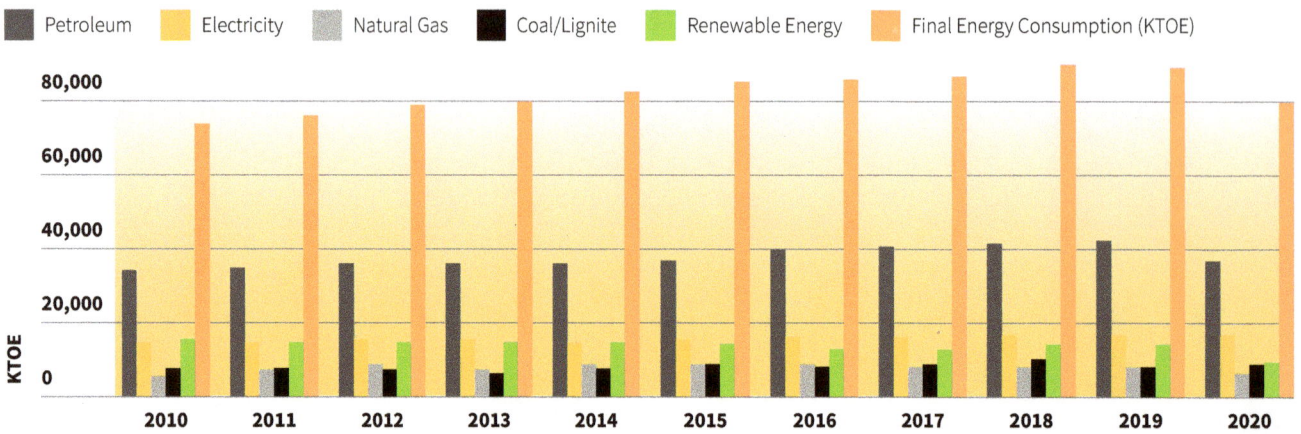

Y-axis: KTOE (0, 20,000, 40,000, 60,000, 80,000)
X-axis: 2010, 2011, 2012, 2013, 2014, 2015, 2016, 2017, 2018, 2019, 2020

Energy Policy and Planning Office (EPPO), 2021

Transportation modes and ancillary infrastructure that produce low or zero direct carbon emissions. This can include national and urban passenger rail and freight rail networks, Bus Rapid Transit (BRT) systems, electric vehicles, and bicycle transport systems.

Sector overview

The final energy consumption of Thailand increased during 2010–2019, before experiencing a slight decrease caused by the impact of the COVID-19 pandemic in 2020.[174] Among different sources of energy, the consumption of petroleum-based products is most dominant (Chart 6). During 2011–2019, natural gas accounted for—on average—66% of electricity generation, followed by coal (18.6%) and oil (6.3%). Renewables—including hydropower, biofuels, and solar PV—occupied a small proportion, approximately 8% (Chart 7).[175] Over the years, Thailand has also relied on hydrocarbon imports in the context of declining domestic crude oil reserves.[176]

Energy security, alternative energy development to reduce reliance on natural gas, energy prices, and moves towards environmental sustainability are the key priorities in Thai energy development policies and strategies.[177] The Alternative Energy Development Plan encourages the development of renewable energy—for instance, from municipal waste, biomass, biogas, wind, and solar—while the PDP2018 sets the target for power generation from renewable energy at 37% by 2037. In 2016, the Government of Thailand adopted the Energy 4.0 policy with Electricity 4.0, Fuel for Transportation 4.0, and Heat 4.0 components.[178] This policy guides the transition to a low carbon economy by boosting renewable energy, energy efficiency, smart energy management, and energy storage capabilities.

Reflecting the policy direction, installed power capacity from renewables continued to increase over the past ten years (Chart 8), from 5,061 megawatts (MW) in 2011 to 11,991 MW in 2020, in comparison with the broader renewable energy target of 19,684 MW by 2036 under the Alternative Energy Development Plan 2015.[179] Bioenergy contributed to 37.5%. of the total power production, while the share of hydropower declined from 30% in 2011 to 25.3% in 2020. The shares of solar photovoltaic (PV) and wind power are smaller than bioenergy and hydropower, but they began to catch up in 2020 with the development of 2,983 MW (solar PV) and 1,507 MW (onshore wind power).[180]

In practice, the PDP2018 has opened more windows for further development of renewable energy in Thailand by promoting new business opportunities for private investment and leveraging modern technologies.[181] Key developments and trends in solar, wind, and waste to energy in the medium term are summarized below:

Solar. Solar energy is the renewable energy source of which Thailand has the most comparative advantage. The northeast and central regions are well suited to develop solar PV systems with high irradiance levels all year round.[182] Solar is the largest expected renewable energy source for electricity generation in the PDP2018. The government subsidy to solar energy through the Feed-in Tariff (FiT) scheme started in 2014. With the target of 15,574 MW under PDP2018, solar power has been strongly promoted by the government and therefore offered clear investment opportunities to investors. New private investments will be in rooftop solar and community solar hybrid projects, and the production of private rooftop solar cells. The power generation capacity is also subject to transmission capacity and suitability of land used for solar energy projects.[183]

Chart 7. Electricity Generation by Source of Energy, 1990–2019

Legend: ■ 1990 ■ 1995 ■ 2000 ■ 2005 ■ 2010 ■ 2015 ■ 2019

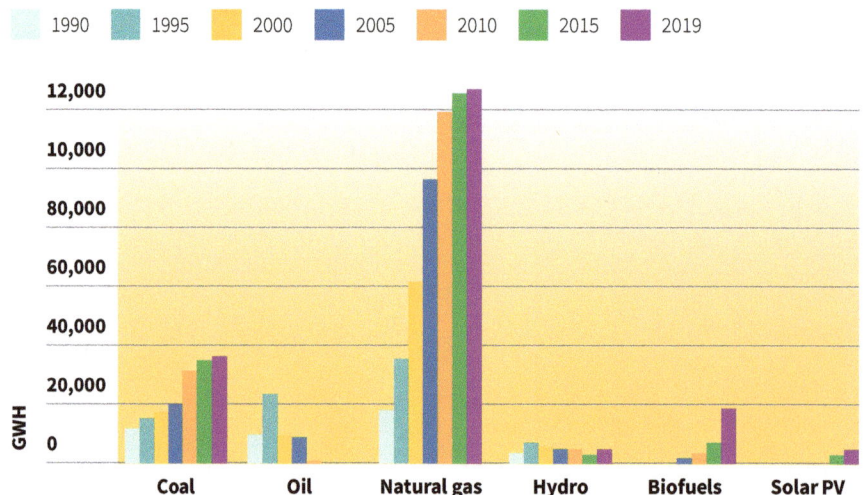

Y-axis: GWH (0, 20,000, 40,000, 60,000, 80,000, 10,000, 12,000)
X-axis: Coal, Oil, Natural gas, Hydro, Biofuels, Solar PV

IEA, Key Energy Indicators[211]

Wind. Wind power has experienced steady growth over the past 5 years. In 2019, installed onshore wind capacity reached 1,507 MW, which is equivalent to 50% of the target set under the PDP2018. At the same time, a 10 MW wind power with a total production capacity of 1.88 megawatt-hour was built in Pak Panang District, Nakhon Si Thammarat Province, by BCPG Public Company Limited, Thailand. This is the first wind farm project equipped with a battery energy storage system, an energy backup system whereby excessive energy is stored and supplied back to the system to maintain the stability and reliability of renewable energy sources.[184] This wind farm model will be expanded to other locations subject to the success of the battery energy storage system.[185] According to Thailand Wind Energy Association, the sector could harness wind energy technologies to enable a potential installed capacity of 13,000–17,000 MW by 2037, which is subject to government wind energy development policy.[186] Investments in wind power projects require capital-intensive investors supported by modern technologies and access to locations suitable for connection with transmission lines.[187] The achievement of the 2036 target for wind (3GW) would depend upon the selected wind turbine technology, including modern low-speed wind turbines, the installation location, and the hub height.[188]

Waste to Energy (WtE). This is a growing investment opportunity. The government will purchase 400 MW of electricity generated from WtE plants in 2022. Electricity from landfill WtE projects qualifies for a FiT of THB5.6/ kilowatt-hour, and power producers of this type of electricity do not need to engage in competitive bidding procedures.[189] *More information on the potential for this sector is provided in the sector overview for Waste Management.*

Financing pathways

Funding for renewable energy and energy efficiency projects in Thailand comes from different sources. Thai commercial banks have extended financing to renewable energy projects, especially solar and wind. The total investment in solar projects reached USD5bn, of which 42% are funded by commercial banks and 41% by project developers' equity during 2008–2017.[190] Siam Commercial Bank, Bangkok Bank, and Kasikorn Bank were the lead financiers for solar and wind projects in Thailand during the period.[191]

Public finance has contributed to energy efficiency and renewable energy investment by financing eligible projects with low-interest loans through the on-lending programme in collaboration with local commercial banks. The credit lines in a range of USD2.50 million–USD10 million were provided to 11 commercial banks during 2003–2012.[192] In 2020, a state budget of THB2bn (USD60 million) was allocated to further support eligible energy efficiency and renewable energy projects.[193]

DFIs such as ADB, the IFC, and multilateral climate funds—such as Climate Investment Funds—have also supported renewable energy in Thailand to engage and leverage private investments. For example, the Thai Clean Technical Fund investment plan is targeting USD300 million in concessional financing to catalyse private investments in renewable energy and energy efficiency and to support direct investments in renewable energy and energy efficiency by state-owned electric utilities and the Bangkok bus rapid transit system.[194]

The growth of the Thai green bond market since 2018 has also benefited renewable energy projects. USD943 million equivalent of green bonds was issued during 2018–2020 to finance the renewable energy and waste

sectors.[195] For instance, in 2018, B. Grimm Power Public Company Limited (B. Grimm Power) issued maiden 5-year and 7-year green bonds—the first certified climate bonds to be issued in Thailand—in which ADB invested THB5bn (USD153 million).[196] This was also the second green bond project under the ADB Green Bond Program.[197] During 2019–2020, more energy companies also issued green bonds for investment in renewable energy and energy efficiency, including Energy Absolute Public Company Limited, PPT Public Company Limited, Global Power Synergy Public Company Limited, and RATCH Public Company Limited.

Chart 8. Thailand's Renewable Power Installed Capacity, 2011–2020

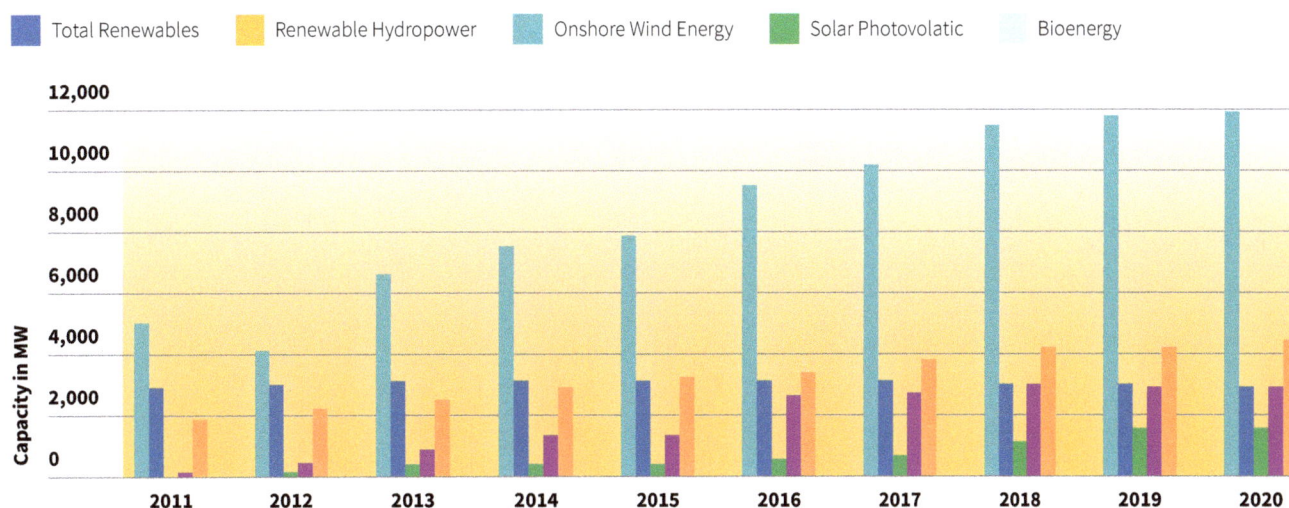

Legend: Total Renewables, Renewable Hydropower, Onshore Wind Energy, Solar Photovolatic, Bioenergy

Source: IRENA, Renewable energy statistics, 2021

Solar PV Project

Proponent: B. Grimm Power Public Company Limited (B. Grimm Power).

Location: Ayutthaya, Pathum Thani, Sakaeo, Chachoengsao, Phetchabun, Surat Thani provinces, and Bangkok, Thailand.

Status: Completed construction, and in commercial operation.

Classification: Renewable energy, Solar PV.

Description: Power production capacity of 98 megawatts (MW) from 16 solar plants. The plant size ranges from 2.3 MW to 8 MW, and the plants are under 25-year power purchase agreements with PEA and MEA under the Very Small Power Producer (VSPP) programme.

Investment costs: USD153 million.

Financial structure: Green bond (USD153 million), 2018, arranged solely by ADB.[212]

Output: With 16 solar PV plants, B. Grimm Power had set the goal to increase the share of renewable power generation from 10% to 30% in its energy portfolio by 2021. As of May 2021, renewable power generation accounts for 28.5% of its portfolio.[213]

Subyai Wind Power Project[214]

Proponent: Chaiyaphum Wind Farm Company Limited.

Location: Subyai District, Chaiyaphum Province, Thailand.

Status: Completed construction, and in commercial operation in 2016.

Classification: Renewable energy, Wind power.

Description: The total contracted capacity of 81 MW, comprising 32 unit wind turbines at 2.5 MW each.

Investment costs: USD200 million.

Financial structure: Blended financing of (i) ADB Direct Loan of USD53.15 million (ii) Clean Technical Fund (CTF) Loan of USD30m, (iii) Loan from the Bank of Ayudhya Public Company Limited of USD67.9 m.; and (iv) Others: Equity financing of USD48.94 m.

Output: At least 120,000 MWh of wind power delivered to the off-taker per annum, and at least 65,000 tons of CO2 equivalent emissions avoided per annum (2016–2026).

Hanuman Wind Farm Project[215]

Proponent: Energy Absolute Public Company Limited.

Location: Chaiyaphum Province in northeastern Thailand.

Status: Completed construction and in commercial operation as of 2019.

Classification: Renewable energy, wind power.

Description: The Hanuman Wind Farm is a collection of five projects split into three clusters of wind turbines with substations in the southwestern part of Chaiyaphum Province. The total generation capacity is 260 MW, consisting of subprojects HNM1 (45 MW), HNM8 (45 MW), HNM5 (48 MW), HNM9 (42 MW), and HNM10 (80 MW).

Investment cost: Total investment: THB2bn.[216]

Refinancing structure: (i) Green bond, THB10bn (USD325.4 million). Green bond was certified by Climate Bonds in 2019, of which ADB investment was THB3bn (USD98.7 million). The bond was used for the long-term financing of the Hanuman Wind Farm (including the refinancing of short-term supplier credit);[217] (ii) Green loan (climate loan certified by Climate Bonds) provided by ADB in 2020; (iii) Others: Equity and other loans. [218]

Output: One of the largest wind power projects in Southeast Asia aimed to (i) meet the strong increase in power production and supply from renewables; (ii) reduce greenhouse gas emissions, and (iii) contribute to the total renewable power production nationwide as the targets set under PDP2018.

Sustainable transport

Sector overview

Environmental sustainability has become an increasingly important consideration in the transport sector in Thailand. Through a short term programme (2013–2017), and a long term plan (2018–2030), the Environmental Sustainable Transport Master Plan (2013) aims to reduce energy intensity, GHG emissions, and air pollution from transport, with the development of public transportation and mass rapid transit systems as one of the key implementation strategies.[219] In 2017, the Government of Thailand—with the support from the German Federal Ministry for the Environment, Nature Conservation and Nuclear Safety (BMU)—implemented the Clean Mobility Programme.[220] To execute this programme, the Thailand Pollution Control Department and the Department of Alternative Energy Development collaborated with the United Nations Environment Programme and the Climate and Clean Air Coalition to implement measures to reduce PM2.5 air pollution levels from transport, including (i) stricter vehicle emission standards; (ii) shifting of 2–3 wheelers in Bangkok from gasoline to electric; and (iii) retrofitting boats and ferries used for public transportation.[221] In 2019, the Ministry of Transport (MoT) published the 20-year Transport System Development Strategy (2018–2037) built on three key pillars: (i) green and safe transport, which includes the use of alternative energy; (ii) inclusivity in transportation for full accessibility to public transport services; and (iii) transport efficiency through improving transport and logistics performance and competitiveness by introducing an intelligent transport system.[222]

In terms of infrastructure investment, the Thailand Transport Investment Action Plan has prioritised sustainable transport projects. The 2017 Action Plan outlined (i) 10 projects for Double Track Rail Network (USD11.67bn); (ii) two projects for Commuter Train (USD4.78bn); (iii) six projects for Mass Transit Development (USD6.32bn); and (iv) one project for public bus procurement and stations (USD64.92 million).[223] In addition, the Thai Board of Investment offers tax and non-tax incentives to domestic and international investors to invest in sustainable transport in Thailand, including rail development.[224, 225]

Financing pathways

Public sustainable transport infrastructure in Thailand has been largely financed by annual state budget allocation, government and SOE borrowings, PPPs, SOE revenues, and infrastructure funds:

Government and SOE lending are the major source of funding for transport infrastructure with 47% in 2015, 63% in 2016, 64% in 2017, and 46% in 2018.[226, 227] Government debt consists of sovereign bonds and term loans; and SOE borrowings include on-lending loans from the Government, SOE bonds, and other corporate debts.[228]

Public–private partnerships (PPP). Private investment in transport has become an integral part of the transport infrastructure project financing scheme, especially for megaprojects.[229] PPP arrangements have progressively increased in the financing composition of transport infrastructure in Thailand, with 6% in 2015, 21% in 2016, 22% in 2017, and 24.85% in 2018.[230, 231]

Thailand Future Fund was established under SEC authority in 2016 and raised funds from public investors in 2017. This provides opportunities for investors to invest in state-owned infrastructure projects and helps promote the development of the capital market. The fund initially invested in rights to receive 45% of the 30-year toll revenue of two expressways managed by the Expressway Authority of Thailand with a total distance of 83.2km.[232]

The green bond market has also played an important role in financing sustainable transport in Thailand. In 2019, BTS Group Holdings Public Company Limited issued a THB13bn (USD413.2 million) green bond to institutional and high net worth investors for financing and refinancing the Mass Rapid Transit Pink Line, and the Mass Rapid Transit Yellow Line Projects, which are qualified as green under Climate Bonds Low Carbon and Land Transport criteria.[233] In 2020, the company issued another THB8.6bn

(USD278 million) green bond for financing and refinancing these same projects, the MRT Pink Line and Yellow Line Projects.[234] In 2020, the Public Debt Management Office (PDMO) in the Ministry of Finance (MoF), also issued the first

sovereign sustainability bond in tabs, with the outstanding size of THB50bn (USD1.67 bn) as of the end of 2020; THB 30 bn (USD1 bn) of the proceeds were allocated to refinance the expansion of the Mass Rapid Transit Orange East Line (electric train), and THB20bn (0.67bn) of the proceeds were allocated for COVID-19 recovery financing.[235] The transport project financed by the bond proceeds met the Low Carbon Transport Climate Bonds Certification Criteria.[236] According to the PDMO Sustainability Bond Interim Report 2020, the Thai government—through PDMO—would issue more sovereign sustainability bonds to reach THB100bn (USD3.2bn) in 2021 for continued investment in—among others—sustainable transport as part of the economic recovery process.[237]

Mass Rapid Transit Pink Line and Yellow Line Projects

Proponent: BTS Group Holdings Public Company Limited.

Location: Bangkok, Thailand.

Status: Started in March 2018 and under construction. The civil works progress was 80.56% (Pink Line: Khoe Rai-Min Buri), and 84.44% (Yellow Line: Lat Phao-Sam Rong) as of July 31, 2021.[238]

Classification: Low carbon and/or sustainable transportation.

Description:

- MRT Pink Line. Covering 35.5 km, the rail project includes the construction of 30 elevated stations integrated into other mass transit lines, with a 118,400 m2 depot at the Min Buri station serving as an interchange between the Pink and Orange transit lines.[239]

- MTR Yellow Line. Covering 30.4 km, the line is being developed from the Ratchada-Lat Phrao intersection southeast to the Samrong, Samut Prakan Province, and will run between Lat Phrao and Samrong.[240]

Investment costs: Pink Line: THB56.7 bn (USD 1.7bn);[241] and Yellow Line: THB54.8 bn.[242,243](USD1.7 bn)

Financing structure: PPP arrangement implemented by a consortium including the BTS Group Holdings Public Company Limited (75%), Sino-Thai Engineering and Construction Public Company Limited (15%), and RATCH Group Public Company Limited (10%). The consortium established two subsidiary companies: Northern Bangkok Monorail Company Limited (NBM), and Eastern Bangkok Monorail Company Limited (EBM). Financing of the total investment costs include: (i) an ADB approved loan package of THB9.9bn (USD311 million) to NBM and EBM for the construction and operation of the Pink and Yellow lines; (ii) loans from commercial banks (Bangkok Bang, Krung Thai Bank, and Siam Commercial Bank)[244,245] and (iii) Others: Equity including BTS Group Holdings' issuance of green bonds: THB13bn (USD413.2 million) (2019) and THB8.6bn (USD273 million) (2020).[246,247]

Output: A cost-effective public transport system, contributing to sustainable transport development objectives.[248]

Mass Rapid Transit Orange East Line

Proponent Mass Rapid Transit Authority of Thailand (SOE).

Location: Bangkok, Thailand.

Status: Under construction (85.33% by August 2021).[249]

Classification: Clean and/or sustainable public transportation.

Description: Greenfield project. A mass rapid transit for electric trains between Thailand Cultural Center and Min Buri (Suwingthawong), which is part of the whole MRT Orange Line with a total length of 35.9 km covering two sections: the eastern and western parts of Bangkok. The eastern section is 22.57 km long with 10 underground stations and seven elevated stations.[250]

Investment cost: THB113.3 bn. (USD3.78 bn.).[251] Civil work construction cost is THB79.2 bn. (USD2.64 bn).[252]

Financing structure: State budget, including proceeds from a sovereign sustainability bond, issued in taps, of THB30 bn to refinance project capital expenditures.[253]

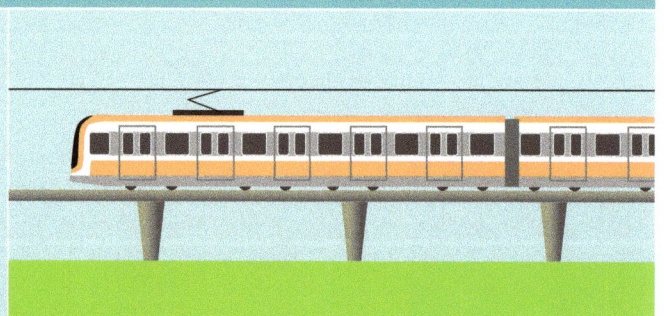

Output: Expansion in public urban transport between western and eastern areas in Bangkok (serving more than 120,000 commuters daily in 2023 and up to 500,000 in 2028).

High-Speed Railway Project connecting Three Airports[254,255]

Proponent: Joint venture between the State Railway of Thailand (SRT) and Asia Era One Company Ltd., (Thailand), representing the consortium of Charoen Pokphand Holding PLC, CH, Karnchang PLC, Bangkok Expressway and Metro PLC, Italian-Thai Development PLC, and China Railway Construction Corporation Ltd.

Location: Bangkok and other provinces, Thailand.

Status: Under construction (2021).

Classification: Clean and/or sustainable public transportation.

Description: High speed rail and airport rail link extension to link the three international airports (Don Mueang, Suvarnabhumi, and U- Tapao) in the Bangkok and vicinity area.

Investment cost: THB258bn (USD7.84bn).[256]

Financing structure: A 50-year PPP contract arrangement implemented by (i) the government (THB158 billion/ USD4.8bn), and (ii) the private sector (THB100bn/USD3.04bn). All infrastructure will be transferred to the government at the end of the concession period.

Output: Low carbon transport connectivity to improve the Eastern Economic Corridor (EEC) corridor and attract international and domestic investments. This project aims to contribute THB650bn (USD19.75bn) to the Thai economy and create 16,000 jobs during the construction period.

Enhance Private Sector Participation in Freight Transportation by Rail (Khon Kaen-Laem Chabang)[257,258]

Proponent: State Railway of Thailand (SRT), Ministry of Transport (MoT).

Location: Chon Buri, Chachoengsao, Saraburi, Nakhon Ratchasima, Khon Kaen, Udon Thani, and Nong Khai provinces, Thailand.

Status: Planned (PPP Delivery Project 2020–2027). The project is at the Government announcement stage.

Classification: Clean and/or sustainable transport (freight and passenger railway).

Description: Project to engage private investments in marketing passenger and freight transportation by rail. The total length of the rail roadway is 683 km. The private sector will operate rail transport services outside SRT operating hours and pay the SRT for use of the rail tracks.

Investment cost: THB26bn (USD790 million).

Financing structure: PPP.

Output: Increased use of freight and passenger transportation by railway, and efficiency and effectiveness of the national railway infrastructure.

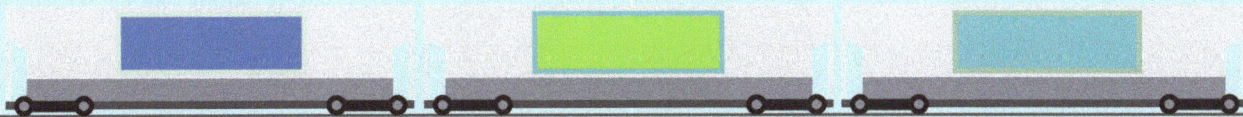

Mass Rapid Transit (MRT) Purple Line (Tao Pun-Rat Burana) Project

Proponent: Mass Rapid Transit Authority of Thailand (MRTA), Ministry of Transport (MoT).

Location: Bangkok, Thailand.

Status: Planned: Inviting tenders subject to international competitive bidding basis for the civil work construction in July 2021.

Classification: Clean and/or sustainable public transport.

Description: The rail system runs a total length of 24.49 km covering Tao Pun-Rat Burana, with 10 underground stations and 7 elevated stations. The project was supported by ADB technical assistance to enhance the project readiness, including due diligence requirements, development of a multimodal transport network integration plan, and capacity building on urban rail operations and maintenance.[259]

Investment cost: THB124.79bn (USD3.79bn).[260]

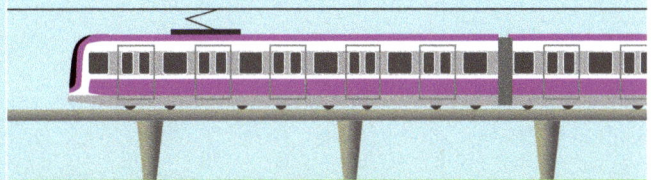

Financing structure: PPP contract arrangements including (i) domestic loan, and (ii) private investments.

Output: Improving low carbon and/or clean urban transport system for the efficient and safe movement of people.

Sustainable water management

Assets that do not increase greenhouse gas emissions or that aim at emission reductions over the operational lifetime of the asset, address adaptation, and increase the resilience of surrounding environments. These assets cover built as well as nature-based water infrastructure.

Water management projects could include water capture and collection, water storage, water treatment (with methane emissions treatment), flood defence, drought defence, stormwater management, and ecological restoration and management.

Sector overview

Sustainable water management has been recognised as one of the national sustainable development goals.[261, 262] The National Water Resources Management Strategy 2015–2026 targets six strategic pillars, including (i) management of water for consumption, (ii) water security in the production sector, (iii) flood and inundation management, (iv) water quality management, (v) rehabilitation of forest watersheds and degraded areas, and (vi) management and institution.[263] The Government of Thailand also ratified a Water Resources Act and the 20-year Master Plan on Water Resources Management 2018–2037, streamlining the National Water Resources Management Strategy 2015–2026 in alignment with the 20-year National Strategy 2018–2037.

To put the master plan into operation, water infrastructure projects on water supply, treatment, storage, water resource management, flood prevention, and control have been proposed, planned, and executed nationwide. Government agencies—including the Ministry of Agriculture and Cooperatives, the Ministry of Environment and Natural Resources, and the Ministry of Industry (MoI)—lead the development of these projects and are supported by metropolitan and provincial waterworks authorities. The Government of Thailand has also encouraged private participation to accelerate the development of water infrastructure projects. The PPP Act 2019 has included water infrastructure as an eligible category for private investments.[264]

Financing pathways

Water infrastructure investments in Thailand are mainly financed by the state budget and borrowings, e.g., concession loans financed by multilateral and bilateral donors, especially for large scale infrastructure projects. PPP is also becoming an important financing tool for the sector. Under the PPA Act, the State Enterprise Policy Office has published the PPP Delivery Plan 2020–2027, which includes water management, irrigation, waterworks, and wastewater treatment projects as priorities.[265] In addition, the EEC Water Supply Development and Management Strategy 2020–2037 covers 53 projects with an investment cost of THB52.80bn (USD1.6bn). These planned projects have also opened new opportunities for private investments.[266] Large scale water infrastructure projects—such as flood defence, and water storage—have been planned to receive national and municipal public funding during 2022–2024.[267]

Investment projects on water monitoring, water storage, flood defence, water distribution, water treatment, and natural-based solutions are eligible for green investments under the Climate Bonds Taxonomy. This implies that green bonds and/or sustainability bonds are well suited to finance these types of projects. Blended finance can also be an effective instrument to mobilize capital and increase the bankability of water infrastructure projects—such as flood protection, drought management, and water quality management—which are important for Thailand to achieve the Sustainable Development Goal (SDG) 6 on water and sanitation.[268, 269]

Thai Tap Water (TTW) Water Production and Distribution Concession Project[270]

Proponent: Mitsui & Co., Ltd., Japan and with Ch. Karnchang Public Company Limited, Thailand.

Location: Nakhon Pathom and Samut Sakhon Provinces, Thailand.

Status: Construction completed (2005). In commercial operation.

Classification: Drinking water supply.

Description: Private Participation in Infrastructure (PPI) Project. TTW supplies drinking water to consumers in Nakhon Pathom and Samut Sakhon provinces. Production capacity is 320,000 m3 per day. TTW entered the agreement on tap water supply with the Provincial Waterworks Authority (PWA) of Thailand for 30 years.

Investment cost: THB8.9bn(USD235 million).[271]

Financing and Refinancing structure: 100% private investment by joint shareholdings.

Output: TTW participation successfully contributed to stable water supply services. The PPI helped release the financial burden of PWA, stabilise water tariff revenue for PWA, and provide sufficient clean water to end users in the two provinces and extended areas.

Lam Nam Chi Reservoir Project[272]

Proponent: Ministry of Agriculture and Cooperatives; Royal Irrigation Department (RID).

Location: Ban Yang Na Di in Ban Khwao District and Ban Han Khai in Nong Bua Rawe District, Chaiyaphum Province, Thailand.

Status: Under construction (2019–2024).

Classification: Water reservoir (flood management and water supply).

Description: The construction project consists of a zone dam and a spillway. Water supply capacity is up to 70.21 million m3 of water.

Investment cost: THB3.1bn (USD100 million).[273]

Financing and Refinancing structure: Public funding.

Output: Tackling the problem of water shortage in the province and the northeast region in Thailand, covering agricultural production of 75,000 rais (30,000 acre s) of farmland in the rainy season, and 30,000 rais (12,000 acres) in the dry season. The project also benefits fishery activities and flood control.

Khlong Toei Wastewater Treatment Facility[274]

Proponent: Bangkok Metropolitan Administration.

Location: Bangkok, Thailand.

Status: Planned (2020–2027).

Classification: Greenfield project: Wastewater Treatment Facility.

Description: Collect and clean 360,000 m3 of wastewater per day, covering 71 km2.

Investment cost: THB12.47bn (USD379 million).

Financing and Refinancing structure: Proposed PPP contract arrangement.

Output: Resolve wastewater problems in the Chao Phraya River and other canals: Saen Saep, Tan, Phra Khanong, Bang Na, Phai Singto, Bang Chak, Toei, and Hua Lamphong.

Construction of the CLS Dam Project and wastewater collection system at Saen Saeb Canal[275]

Proponent: Bangkok Metropolitan Administration.

Location: Bangkok, Thailand.

Status: Planned (2022–2026).

Classification: Sustainable water management.

Description: A system of a dam and wastewater collection between Min Buri Nong Chok sluices, a reinforced concrete water reservoir with a capacity of 479,500 m3.

Investment cost: THB1.8bn (USD54.7 million).[276]

Financing structure: Public funding: (i) 50% by Bangkok Metropolitan Administration; and (ii) 50% government budget.

Output: Improve the drainage system in the Saen Saep canal, control water pollution, and prevent flooding in a 90 km2 area covering Klong Sam Wa, Min Buri and Nong Chok areas.[277]

♲ Sustainable waste management

The efficient use of resources to cut down on waste production, coupled with collection and disposal systems that promote reuse and recycle, thereby minimising residual waste going into energy from waste facilities. Where waste must go to landfill, there are gas capture systems installed to minimise emissions as well as measures to minimise run-off and other negative impacts on surrounding environ ments.

Sector overview

In Thailand, waste generation averages 1.13 kg per capita per day, leading to 27.8 million tons of solid waste produced per year.[278, 279] In the Bangkok Metropolitan Region, plastic waste accounts for 20% of the total of 10,500 tons of waste per day, of which only 25% is recycled.[280] Thailand averages plastic waste generation of 74 kg per capita per year, which is much higher than the world average of 29 kg in 2018. In general, plastic waste is not fully and properly collected and managed, and as result about 336,000 tons of plastics leak to the oceans annually, amounting to 4.8 kg per capita per year.[281] Compared to energy, agriculture, and transport, the waste GHG emissions remained small, but steadily increased from 10.83 tons of carbon dioxide equivalent in 2010 to 12.58 tons of carbon dioxide equivalent in 2016. Reducing GHG emissions from waste in Thailand is part of the sustainable development objectives and international climate commitments.[282]

The Government of Thailand has taken environmental problems from solid waste generation into consideration more than ever before, especially as the country is adopting the circular economy approach. The Twelfth National Economic and Social Development Plan (2017–2021) sets the target of 75% of total solid waste to be properly disposed of or recycled by 2021, while also promoting environmentally friendly products and sustainable production and consumption. The Bio–Circular–Green (BCG) Economy Model Strategic Plan, 2021–2026 recognises sustainable waste management as an important measure to tackle waste generation and achieve a bio-based economy.[283] Thailand also developed the Municipal Solid Waste (MSW) Management Master Plan 2016–2021, which focuses on waste minimisation by applying the Reduce–Reuse–Recycle (3Rs) principle, integrated waste management technologies (such as waste to energy (WTE), biogas, and material recovery), and clustering municipality areas. The master plan also promotes PPPs to encourage private sector participation in MSW management.[284] Recently, the Government has also approved the Roadmap on Plastic Waste Management 2018–2030 with an ambition to recycle all plastic waste by 2027.[285]

With the implementation of the mid-term and long-term government policy frameworks, Thailand has experienced many achievements in waste management. The clustering approach has created an aggregation effect on MSW management, resulting in economies of scale and cost efficiency in operating MSW management systems. As a policy instrument, PPPs have opened more investment opportunities for the private sector in the waste sector, especially in large-scale waste management projects. At the same time, the expansion of WtE model for power generation from waste disposal systems has contributed to power generation capacity as planned in the PDP2018. To promote more investment in waste management, the Board of Investment of Thailand offers incentive schemes to encourage investment in the use of secondary raw materials, waste recycling, and sustainable production technologies as part of a strategy to achieve its BCG economic model.[286] Despite progress, many issues need further consideration from the Government, including public policies on small sized waste management projects (investment cost less than THB5bn (USD150 million), and the continued increase in plastic, hazardous, and electronic waste generation and associated public health concerns.[287]

Financing pathways

In addition to public funding, green banking programmes, PPPs, corporate green bonds, and mezzanine financing (debt and equity) are the prevalent financing mechanisms for investment in sustainable waste management in Thailand. PPP modalities have been established for investment in the waste sector in Thailand since 2014 and were subsequently reformed in compliance with the PPP Act 2019 to mobilize resources from the private sector for investment in waste management operating systems. Many PPP waste management projects have been successfully implemented in Thailand. For example, Rayong Provincial Administrative Organization has been cooperating with Global Power Synergy Public Company Limited (GPSC) to operate the Rayong Waste to Energy Project since 2018.[288]

Green bonds have also become a financing instrument for the sector in recent years. In 2018, IFC invested USD60 million in the first green bond issued by the TMB Bank as part of the IFC Climate Finance Programme which supports investment in renewable energy, energy efficiency, and sustainable waste management. With continued support from the IFC, TMB Bank plans to increase its green financing programme from USD280 million to USD470 million during 2018–2023.[289] In 2020, Global Power Synergy Public Company Limited (GPSC), issued a THB5bn (USD160.5 million) corporate green bond to the Thai capital market for investments in renewable energy and waste projects (50:50 funding ratio by sector).[290] Given the important role that the waste sector could play in the marine plastic agenda, Thailand may consider issuing blue bonds to tackle the critical pollution issue caused by plastic waste released to the sea in near future (Box 3).

Integrated Waste Management Project[291]

Proponent: Global Power Synergy Public Company (GPSC) Limited and Rayong Provincial Organization (PAO).

Location: Rayong Province, Thailand.

Status: In commercial operation as of 2018.

Classification: Waste management (WtE).

Description: MSW is treated by waste-to-energy technology, an integrated processes including waste sorting, recycling, and soil amendment. The Rayong PAO is responsible for gathering MSW from the local administrative organisations and supplying 500 tons of MSW to the project per day. GPSC has also invested in a refuse-derived fuel (RDF) power plant for clean power generation in connectivity with this project.

Investment costs: THB600 million (USD18.6 million).[292]

Financing and Refinancing Structure: PPP contract between GPSC and the Rayong PAO for 22 years.

Output: An integrated waste management project in the waste sector with the main contribution being a reduction in environmental and social impacts caused by MSW. It has also increased the capacity of renewable power with the WtE technology.

Waste to Energy Power Plant[293,294]

Proponent: Global Power Synergy Public Company Limited (Subsidiary: Thai Jurong Engineering Limited, Bangkok).

Location: Amphur Mueang, Rayong Province, Thailand.

Status: Completed construction in Q1 2021, and is in commercial operation.

Classification: WtE–Power generation by incineration.

Description: With a power generation capacity of 9.8 MW, the plant is connected to the refuse-derived fuel (RDF) production plant. The produced RDF will be used as fuel for the incinerator power generation.[295] GPSC entered a PPA with the Provincial Electricity Authority (PEA) under the Municipal Waste to Energy Project under the FiT scheme.

Investment cost: THB1.6bn (USD51.36 million), 100% private investment by GPSC.

Financing structure. The Plant is financed by GPSC, including the use of proceeds from a green bond (THB5 billion/ USD160.5 million) issuance from August 2020 (38% for pollution prevention and control, and 62% for renewable energy).

Output: The WtE power plant targeted the reduction of waste from the landfill in Rayong and clean power generation. The capacity in 2021 can cover the energy consumption of 6,700 households.[296] It was expected that the model of the RDF power plant would be further developed to comprehensively handle waste management in Thailand.

Waste Management Project in Phuket, Thailand[297]

Proponent: PJT Technology Co., Ltd (Thailand) and Phuket City Municipality.

Location: Phuket Province, Thailand.

Status: In operation as of 2012.

Classification: MSW management.

Description: MSW is treated by WtE technology by the 700 ton solid waste incinerator plant, with a power generation capacity of 12 MW. The Phuket Municipality is responsible for collecting and transporting waste to the disposal complex for processing. The plant can accommodate the disposal services of 18 local governments in Phuket.

Investment costs: THB940 million (USD30.3million) (initial cost by PJT).

Financing and Refinancing Structure: PPP contract signed between PJT Technology Co., Ltd and the Phuket Municipality. The company invested in construction and is operating the system.

Output: Provision of an environmental solution to MSW management in Phuket with the use of WtE incineration as the robust technology, with public participation in waste reduction and waste separation.

SUEZ Plastic Recycling Plant, Thailand[298]

Proponent: SUEZ, France.

Location: Bang Phli District, Bangkok, Thailand.

Status: In commercial operation as of 2020.

Classification: Plastic recycling (waste management).

Description: The plant converts 30,000 tons of plastic packaging waste per year into post-consumer recycled plastic. The plant is also equipped with a high-tech treatment system to maximise water reuse of recycling plants (94%). The plant is supported by advanced technologies applied to plastic recycling—low-density polyethylene and linear low-density polyethylene—in compliance with European environmental standards.

Investment costs: N/A.

Financing and Refinancing structure: Private investment.

Output: Provision of innovative solutions for plastic pollution in Thailand, and reduction in GHG emissions (manufacturing 1 tonne of recycled plastic can save 5 barrels of oil).

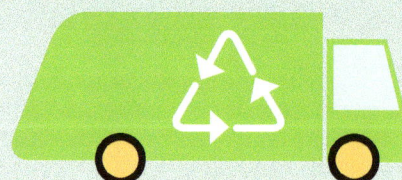

Chonburi Clean Energy Plant (CCE), Thailand[299]

Proponent: A joint venture between Glow Energy Public Company Limited (a subsidiary of France-based ENGIE), SUEZ Environment, and WHA Energy Company Limited to establish Chonburi Clean Energy (CCE), a Thailand–based company.

Location: Hemraj Chonburi Industrial Estate, in the Eastern Economic Corridor (EEC), Thailand.

Status: In operation as of December 2019.

Classification: WtE–Power generation.

Description: Capacity of conversion of 400 tons of industrial waste into electricity per day, equivalent to 100,000 tons per year, with a power generation capacity of 8.63 MW. Waste Management Siam Co., Ltd. is contractually responsible for supplying 100,000 tons of industrial waste collected from WHA industrial in Chonburi and nearby areas to the EEC. The plant uses sustainable waste incineration technology to convert waste into superheated steam that will in turn propel a turbine to generate electricity. In December 2019, CCE entered a PPA with the Provincial Electricity Authority (PEA) for the contracted capacity of 6.9 MW under a 20-year timeframe.

Investment cost: USD59.3 million by Joint venture shareholdings, 33.33% each.

Output: CCE aims to reduce GHG emissions and increase the production of power from renewable sources.

Other green investment sectors

Green Buildings

More investment towards green buildings is central to achieve Thai energy efficiency and climate policy goals. Globally, buildings accounted for 36% of final energy use in 2018.[300] In Thailand, buildings account for roughly 7.6% of CO_2 emissions.[301] In Chiang Mai city, for example, the top three emitters from energy consumption in 2015 came from buildings in the residential, industrial, commercial, and government sectors.[302] As energy demand growth in Thailand is still largely met with oil and natural gas, retrofitting buildings, increasing energy efficiencies, and ensuring that newly constructed buildings are green will be important to reduce GHGs and increase cost saving.

A landmark energy efficiency regulation was introduced in 1992 known as the Energy Conservation Promotion Act. The act led to the creation of the Energy Conservation (ENCON) fund which came into force in 1995. In 2009, the Building Energy Code (BEC) was introduced as a ministerial regulation under the 1992 Act. BEC sets the minimum energy efficiency standards for new and renovated buildings.[303] The Energy Efficiency Plan sets out the national roadmap to carry out these regulations. The Energy Efficiency Plan 2015–2036—the latest plan updated in 2015—has established a goal to achieve a 30% energy intensity reduction by 2036.[304] The plan also aims to reduce the intensity of the building and household sectors by 12%. Since the BEC, multiple green building certification schemes emerged to complement and support the growth of the green building market. There are multiple green building certification options for developers to choose from. Leadership in Energy and Environmental Design (LEED), Green Mark, and the Thailand Rating of Energy and Environmental Sustainability (TREES) are the most widely used green building labelling schemes in Thailand.[305] The Electricity Generating Authority of Thailand (EGAT) No. 5 energy efficiency label—which defines the energy performance of relevant building systems,—and the recently introduced eco-village standard—which takes a more holistic approach to the environmental performance of a building—are also relevant to green buildings in Thailand.[306]

The green building and sustainable real estate markets in Thailand are expected to continue growing.[307] As of 2021, there are approximately 245 certified green buildings in Thailand,[308] although the actual number of green buildings is higher.[309] Increased awareness around green building and supportive regulatory frameworks have supported the expansion of the sustainable building market. Office and commercial buildings dominate the green building market in Thailand. Together, they accounted for 73.7% of the certified green building share in 2017. Residential buildings only accounted for 10.5% of the certified green building share.[310] This share is expected to increase in the future as the National Housing Authority (NHA) rolled out a green housing programme for low-income communities in 2017.[311] In 2018, the Government of Thailand submitted two Nationally Appropriate Mitigation Actions (NAMA) to the UNFCCC that specifically target greening low-income housing and government buildings.[312] Greening the entire 639 targeted government buildings could remove up to 98,808 tCO2 per year.[313]

While many of the green residential buildings are funded by multilateral funders such as ADB, the IFC,[314] and the Global Environment Facility, the increasing number of projects in the green residential building pipeline opens the opportunity to attract more green financing through green loans and green bonds.[315] Green bonds have been widely used to finance green buildings in ASEAN. 48.6% of total ASEAN green bonds proceeds were used towards financing green buildings, representing the second largest sector financed via green bonds, after energy.[316] In partnership with ADB, the NHA is currently preparing the pipeline for building green housing projects for its sustainability bond issuance.[317] Green buildings also have the potential to drive the growth of green loans. UOB Bank recently extended a green loan to Asia Capital Real Estate to finance its green residential rental apartment complex in Phuket.[318] Their residential apartment projects comply with EDGE green building standards and are expected to reduce 40% of energy and water usage compared to conventional housing.[319]

Smart cities

Climate smart investments in cities will not only protect cities from climate-related disasters but will also contribute to reducing GHG emissions in line with the Paris Agreement climate goals. Thailand currently is propelling its smart cities initiative through the Thailand 4.0 Roadmap. The EEC is a flagship project for the smart city plans of Thailand and the BCG economic model is adopted for projects under the EEC to integrate sustainability into smart cities.[320] This model will translate into new green investment opportunities in city infrastructure that focuses on reducing industrial carbon emissions (such as smart transport), improving energy efficiency, and optimizing resource management for waste and water infrastructure.[321] Thailand has a goal to increase its BCG investment to USD147bn by 2025, tripling the BCG investment values at 2020.[322]

Apart from the BCG concept, new investments in digitisation and smart technologies in Thailand can also strengthen urban decarbonisation efforts.[323] In September 2021, Thailand announced a plan to develop 10 more areas into smart cities, these include three areas in Bangkok, two in Chiang Mai, and one each in Trang, Yala, Chachoengsao, Chon Buri, and Nakhon Sawan. The areas will see improvements to their digital infrastructure, which bring improvements to the economy, mobility, energy use, and the environment.[324]

Coastal Management

Thailand is highly vulnerable to coastal risks of climate change and is already experiencing threats from coastal erosion. In 2018, 30% of the coastlines were at critical levels of erosion with more than 5 metres of erosion per year.[325] Land subsidence, land use change from aquaculture and residential expansion, and mass tourism are all driving coastal erosion in Thailand.[326, 327] Climate change is also exacerbating these erosions through its effects on sea level rise and intensified storms.[328] Without sufficient investment in climate-resilient coastal infrastructure, the population living along the coastlines will be heavily affected by storm surges and saline intrusion into freshwater from sea level rise.[329] Cities will also be affected. Sea level rise, land subsidence, and the potential of cyclone-induced storm surges already puts Bangkok at risk.[330] Investing in sustainable coastal management projects—especially those that strengthen nature-based coastal infrastructure such as rivers and wetlands (marshes and mangroves), and coral reefs—is proven to be an effective solution for climate change adaptation and resilience, as they provide effective natural protection from high tides, storm surges, and flooding.[331] Investment in mangroves also helps with carbon sequestration (mangroves sequester more carbon than terrestrial forests), thus contributing to climate mitigation objectives.

The Nationally Determined Contribution (NDC) has established mangrove restoration and expansion of forest cover as a key climate change adaptation strategy.[332] Even though Thailand had lost 56% of its mangrove cover during 1961–1996, the effects from coverage loss were mitigated by the government policy shift from mangrove exploitation towards mangrove conservation and restoration since 1998.[333] During 2002–2012, the rate of mangrove loss was significantly slower in Thailand compared to other Southeast Asian countries.[334] Thailand has also been uniquely successful in implementing community-based mangrove management that can be largely attributed to internal community capacity

and government support and promotion of community-based models.[335]

While strong policy measures to expand mangrove restoration exist, there is still under-investment in sustainable coastal management projects involving nature-based solutions, particularly when compared to the extensive ecosystem benefits they bring, especially in avoiding long-term physical and financial losses.[336] The global financial flow towards coastal protection is quite scant, accounting for only 1% of total global climate finance flows in 2018.[337] Globally, USD11.1 bn is required over the next 20 years to restore global mangroves[338], while investments in conservation projects needs to be at least 20 to 30 times greater than today, reaching USD 200-300 bn per year.[339] In Thailand, more investment in sustainable coastal management projects—particularly in the mangrove areas—presents a promising opportunity to promote green COVID-19 recovery with strong involvement from coastal communities, while contributing to both climate adaptation and mitigation goals under the NDC. Blue bonds and loans can be used to finance projects that enhance sustainable use of ocean resources in Thailand for economic development (Box 3).

Box 3: Blue Bonds

Oceans and marine ecosystems are crucial for climate change mitigation and adaptation, but they are constantly threatened by coastal deforestation, coral reef extinction, habitat losses, plastic pollution, sea level rise, currents, temperature, water chemistry, over-exploitation, invasive species, and biodiversity loss. Protecting marine resources could bring more returns than their exploitation. For example, it is estimated that a live shark in the Galapagos can generate more than USD5 million in tourism; however, a marketed dead shark only generated USD280.[340] Yet, SDG 14 (Life below water) is the UN SDG that has received the least amount of investment so far.[341]

Many economic sectors operate ocean-based activities and are therefore exposed to the negative impacts from the degradation of oceans and marine ecosystems. These sectors include tourism, fisheries and aquaculture, biotechnology, offshore energy, and marine aggregates. Within these sectors, there are opportunities for issuing blue bonds to finance investments that reduce negative environmental impacts from ocean-based activities. However, many ocean-based activities do not have well defined property rights, and impacts tend to be difficult to be tracked. Therefore, blue finance so far is more likely to be pushed forward by public institutions. The world's first blue bond, for example, was issued in 2018 by the Republic of Seychelles. The bond was a USD15 million private placement bond, structured with support from the World Bank, and aimed to finance the expansion of marine protected areas, improve fisheries governance, and develop the blue economy of the archipelago.

Blue economy projects can have higher financing costs related to small markets, infrastructural deficiencies, and higher risks associated with their direct exposure to climate change. Therefore, measures to improve public and private institutional capacities to manage, reduce, and compensate risks associated with coastal and ocean assets are crucial to help reduce these costs.

In 2019, ADB launched the Action Plan for Healthy Oceans and Sustainable Blue Economies, committing to expand to USD5bn investments and technical assistance within these areas until 2024.[342] The plan focuses on four main areas: (i) developing sustainable tourism and fisheries; (ii) protecting and restoring coastal and marine ecosystems; (iii) controlling pollution; and (iv) improving sustainable port and coastal infrastructure. Along with the plan, the ADB Oceans Financing Initiative accelerates blue investments and supports member countries to finance sustainable projects by (i) proposing detailed principles, criteria, and indicators for blue finance frameworks; (ii) developing innovative and bankable projects with governments and partners; (iii) supporting the development of innovative mechanisms to reduce risks of blue instruments; and (iv) increasing access to financing options from ADB.

In November 2020, ADB and Indorama Ventures Public Company Limited (IVL) signed a USD100 million financing package to reduce the environmental impact of plastic and promote a circular economy by boosting the capacity of IVL plastic recycling plants in India, Indonesia, the Philippines, and Thailand. The plants will recycle polyethylene terephthalate plastics widely used in beverage bottles. This is the first independently verified non-sovereign blue loan by ADB, following Blue Natural Capital Financing Facility Blue Bond Guidelines, with an assurance report from DNV. It is aligned with the ADB Action Plan for Healthy Oceans and Sustainable Blue Economies. The total finance package comprises USD50 million from ADB and USD50 million from the ADB-administered Leading Asia's Private Infrastructure Fund, USD150 million from the IFC, and USD50 million from Deutsche Investitions- und Entwicklungsgesellschaft mbH.[343]

Section 4. Measures for growing green infrastructure

Sections 2 and 3 show that Thailand has seen a steady increase in green infrastructure investment, with a growing number of low-emission and climate resilient infrastructure projects in various sectors. The projects described in the case studies have generated both environmental benefits and new economic opportunities, including new green jobs. To support this expanding portfolio of green infrastructure investment, Thailand has been able to utilise the green bond and/or sustainability bond markets to mobilize capital. Issuing these bonds allows Thailand to incorporate environmental and social indicators in infrastructure investment while meeting investors' growing enthusiasm and expectations for sustainable and low carbon products. This development has been strongly supported by laws, policies, and strategies which guide both overall national development (such as the Thailand 4.0 initiative, targeting the development of a bio, circular, and green (BCG) economy), and sector development priorities (such as climate change, energy, transport, sustainable finance).

The growth of green infrastructure pipelines and associated green finance (including the green bond market) in Thailand can be further leveraged by key policy and institutional changes. Such measures should raise the profile of green infrastructure, support critical finance channels for infrastructure development stakeholders, diversify risks and create more options for investors. Key measures to consider include:

i. Accelerate the implementation of key measures identified in the Sustainable Finance Initiatives in Thailand:[344]

a. A national sustainable finance taxonomy.
The taxonomy will provide a common language on green investment to classify financial flows from investors to project developers. The taxonomy is also an important tool to enhance the visibility of the green infrastructure project pipeline to both domestic and international investors. It will also contribute to enhancing the objectivity of ESG verification methodologies, and developing more innovative financial products and services such as green loans, bonds, and index-linked capital market products etc. It is important, however, that Taxonomy efforts are harmonised with international taxonomies and the global trend towards a common ground definition (such as the International Platform on Sustainable Finance).

b. An ESG database and information disclosure mechanism.
The mechanism will help systematize ESG data produced by green infrastructure project owners and enhance access to such information by investors and financial institutions. Disclosure and reporting play an important role in building green and/or sustainable market confidence and value.

ii. Establish a green project preparation facility

Thailand may also benefit from a **green infrastructure finance facility (GIFF)** or a **green project preparation facility (GPPF),** as part of a long term measure to develop green infrastructure. When established, the GIFF/GPPF can build capacity for government agencies and private stakeholders to produce project preparation documents with high quality standards. A project preparation facility can support pre-feasibility studies and feasibility studies, detailed engineering design, and environmental and social impact assessments. The GIFF/GPPF modality responds to the needs of the country and project developers for technical assistance and advisory services to apply innovative technology and ESG standards, and broader sustainability criteria to project preparation, especially for large-scale infrastructure projects. This will lead to the development of more a bankable and investment-ready infrastructure project pipeline that can attract private investment.

iii. Enact the Thailand Climate Change Act

As the highest legal framework for climate actions, the Thailand Climate Change Act should be enacted to fully mainstream climate change into government policies and strategies across sectors. The Climate Change Act (which is expected to come into effect in 2022)[345] can be a key driver—as well as a governance framework—for all green development, including the infrastructure sector. The Act can also drive further policy support for mainstreaming green and sustainable products in the financial market of Thailand. In the long run, the Act can also have the effect of accelerating actions towards net zero by 2065 announced by Thailand at the COP26, as well as promoting the incorporation of climate risk exposure into new infrastructure plans, accounting for future depreciation of assets due to change in precipitation patterns, temperature increases, and extreme weather events.

Continued awareness-raising and visibility of green investment opportunities for market stakeholders

Training, roadshows, and campaigns can help asset owners and investors understand that there is a sufficiently large opportunity from financially attractive investments that are also green. It will also help consolidate green investments as an effective tool towards building a more resilient economy.

Annexes I and II. Green Debt and Equity Instruments

Debt Instrument	Definition	Example
Supra-national green bonds	Proceeds are allocated to nominated projects and assets. Debt securities carry the credit rating of the issuing State. However, an independent rating may be assigned by ratings agencies.	In the Philippines, the bond, dubbed "Mabuhay bond" is the first peso-denominated, internationally rated triple-A, issued by International Finance Corporation (IFC), a multilateral bank.[346] The PHP4.8bn (USD98.9 million) proceeds will go to repair the Malitbog Geothermal Power station that was damaged due to an earthquake. This project is owned by local renewable energy developer Energy Development Corporation, in Kananga city in Leyte Province.[347] This instrument has not yet been used in Thailand
Sovereign green bonds	Proceeds are allocated to nominated projects and assets. Debt securities carry the credit rating of the issuing State. However, an independent rating may be assigned by ratings agencies.	The Kingdom of Thailand—via its Public Debt Management Office (PDMO)—issued a sovereign sustainability bond in taps totalling THB85bn (USD3.45bn).[348] The proceeds have both green and social components, financing green infrastructure through the Mass Rapid Transit Orange Line (East) Project, as well as social impact projects to assist with COVID-19 recovery, such as public health measures, job creation programmes, and local public infrastructure development, with related social and environmental benefits.[349]
Sub-sovereign green bonds	Proceeds are allocated to nominated projects and assets within the sponsoring region. Credit rating is based on that of the issuing municipality and the credit quality of the underlying assets.	In 2016, the Viet Nam Ministry of Finance approved a pilot project for municipal green bonds. In September the People's Committee of Ba Ria Vung Tau Province came to market with a VND80 billion (USD4 million) 5-year green bond to finance a water resource management project. Shortly after, Ho Chi Minh City Finance and Investment State-owned enterprise issued a VND523.5 billion (USD23 million) 15-year green bond with proceeds allocated to 11 projects related to the water, adaptation, and infrastructure sectors. This instrument has not yet been used in Thailand
General obligation green bond	Proceeds are allocated to nominated projects and assets within the sponsoring region. The bond will carry the credit rating of the issuing entity.	TMB Bank in Thailand issued a USD60 million 7-year green bond in June 2018.[350] Proceeds will be allocated to solar, waste to energy, biomass, and bagasse projects.[351]
Green revenue bond	Proceeds are allocated on nominated projects and assets linked with a municipal government. As the green bonds are backed at least partially by the specific revenue streams (most often tax receipts, lease fees, or other receivables) bonds with no recourse to the issuer	In 2017, Beijing Enterprises Water Group, which operates 19 water treatment plants under contracts with 16 municipalities, issued a securitisation backed by water treatment service fee receivables. The proceeds are to be invested in 9 new water infrastructure projects. This instrument has not yet been used in Thailand
Green structured finance (senior secured)	Debt securities backed by a pool of underlying assets. Proceeds are allocated only to nominated projects and assets. The credit risk is dependent on the asset risks.	In April 2021, Toyota Leasing (Thailand) Co (TLT)—the largest automotive leasing company in the country—successfully issued a senior secured green bond worth THB2bn to finance and refinance TLT's selected hybrid vehicle portfolio. The eligible category for use of clean transport aligns with the Green Bond Principles 2018. The 2-year, 1-month debenture sized at THB2bn is fully guaranteed by Toyota Motor Finance (Netherlands) B.V., a company rated A+ by S&P and A1 by Moody's, with a stable outlook.[352, 353]
Green securitisation Green tranches in ABS and MBS deals	Debt securities backed by a pool of underlying assets. Proceeds are allocated only to nominated projects and assets. Often an independent credit rating is issued by a rating agency, but this is not a requirement. The credit risk is dependent on the asset risks.	FlexiGroup (Australia) has closed three ABS deals with green tranches, mostly senior (Class A), for the refinancing of solar rooftops. Its 2018 deal contained a B note too. Harvest Capital (People's Republic of China) has issued Green CMBS secured on a LEED Gold Certified office building owned by China Energy Conservation and Environmental Protection Group (CECEP). This instrument has not yet been used in Thailand

(continued)

Debt Instrument	Definition	Example
Green convertible bond	Proceeds are allocated on nominated projects and assets. The security can be converted into a predetermined amount of the company common stock. The bond will carry the credit rating of the issuing entity.	Japan-based Sumitomo Forestry Co., Ltd issued the first green convertible in September 2018 to refinance the acquisition of 30,000 hectares (~74,000 acres) of FSC certified timberlands and plantation forests in Nelson, New Zealand. The Stock Acquisition Rights give bondholders the option to acquire company common stock. This instrument has not yet been used in Thailand
Green project bond	Proceeds are allocated on nominated projects and assets. Credit rating is based on the quality of the backing green assets and the returns stream of the underlying project.	In 2019, Energy Absolute PCL of Thailand issued a THB10bn green bond to refinance its 260 megawatt (MW) Hanuman Wind Farm in Chaiyaphum Province in northeastern Thailand. The wind farm has 103 turbines and is one of the largest wind farms in Southeast Asia. The issuance is also the second Climate Bonds Standard-certified bond issued by a Thai energy company and the first to concern a wind project in the country.[354, 355]
Environmental impact bonds and/or pay-for-results green bonds	Proceeds allocated to nominated green projects and/or assets. Part of the project risk is transferred from the issuer to investors. The payments to investors are conditional to the project achieving an expected outcome after a third-party evaluation has been conducted.	DC Water and Sewer Authority issued a USD25 million private placement in 2016 to finance the construction of green infrastructure designed to mimic natural processes to absorb and slow surges of stormwater during periods of heavy rainfall. If the outcome of the project meets expectations, no contingent payment will be due to investors. If it exceeds expectations, investors will make a risk payment share of USD3.3 million to DC Water, if it does not achieve expectations, DC Water will make an outcome payment to investors. 30 US cities of Atlanta and Baltimore recently announced plans to issue environmental impact bonds in 2019. This instrument has not yet been used in Thailand
Private Placement	Green bond placed directly with the investor(s). Details of the deal such as pricing and maturity may remain confidential, but the issuer is expected to disclose details on the nominated projects and assets to be financed.	Thailand-based TMB Bank issued a USD60 million 7-year green private placement in June 2018 to finance solar, biomass, and waste to energy projects. The IFC was the sole investor in the deal.[356] The 2018 B. Grimm Power (THB85bn) was also a private placement.[357]
Green loans, syndicated loans, and credit lines	Provide lending to encourage market development in climate-aligned sectors in line with the Climate Bonds Taxonomy and in compliance with Green Loan Principles. Interest rates are based on borrower credit scores or an ESG score assigned by an ESG rating agency.	In January 2021, Asia Capital Real Estate obtained a THB675 million green loan from the UOB Thailand under the its Real Estate Sustainable Finance Framework to develop HOMA Phuket Town. It is an environmentally friendly affordable residential rental apartment complex in Phuket which is designed to obtain both an EDGE Advanced and a LEED certification upon completion in October 2021.[358] In 2020, ADB also supported Energy Absolute through a green loan.[359]
Mezzanine and subordinated debt	Proceeds are allocated on nominated projects and assets. Hybrid capital investments, from development banks seeking to support private investment in the senior debt or from investors with a higher risk appetite.	Global investment manager AMP Capital provided a EUR245 million mezzanine finance facility of EUR245 million to Neoen, a French renewable energy provider. In May 2018, Canadian insurance company Manulife Financial issued a CAD600 million (USD464 million) 10-year green subordinated secured bond. This instrument has not yet been used in Thailand

Credit enhancement mechanisms	Definition	Example
Full or partial credit guarantee (PCG)	A credit guarantee or PCG is created to absorb part or all the debt service default risk of an infrastructure project, irrespective of the cause of default. PCGs can be used for any commercial debt instrument (loans, bonds) from a private lender. The existence or proposed implementation of a PCG is indicative of confidence in the product being floated by the guaranteeing entity and can even assist in bringing new lenders to the table.	The Nationally Appropriate Mitigation Actions facility (NAMA facility) is a multi-donor fund established by Germany (BMUB) and the UK (BEIS) to support developing countries and emerging economies in implementing ambitious actions to mitigate greenhouse gas emissions.[360] Thailand is among the countries obtaining support from this facility. Within Thailand, the NAMAs facility provides a partial credit guarantee to energy efficiency projects. Specifically, a guaranteed mechanism will improve the bankability for ESCOs and energy end-users wishing to implement EE projects.[361]
Partial risk guarantee and/or Political risk guarantee	PRGs cover private lenders and investors for certain risks of lending to sovereign or sub-sovereign borrowers. A PRG needs to include private participation in the project. A PRG can cover several sovereign or sub-sovereign risks such as currency inconvertibility, repatriation, expropriation, political force majeure such as war, regulatory risk, and government payment obligations (such as tariffs).	On December 31, 2015, the Multilateral Investment Guarantee Agency (MIGA) issued a USD39.7 million guarantee to several lenders, led by Goldman Sachs and Bank of Tokyo Mitsubishi. The loan was guaranteed by the Ministry of Finance—acting for and on behalf of the Government of Viet Nam—to support the construction of the Hoi Xuan Hydropower Plant in Thanh Hoa, Viet Nam. The plant was to produce and sell electricity to the national utility company, Viet Nam Electricity (EVN), under a power purchase agreement. The guarantee covered the risk of non-honouring of sovereign financial obligations concerning the government repayment guarantee to the lenders with a tenor of 15 years. This instrument has not yet been used for green projects in Thailand
Partial risk swap guarantees	Partial Swap Guarantees cover investors against the risks arising from currency swaps in cross-border transactions or where the debt service cash flow is in a different currency from the deal cash flows, which would require the issuer to hedge the currency mismatch to provide comfort to investors that payments can be made in the debt currency.	Brazil-based private bank Unibanco issued JPY25 billion 10-year amortising notes backed by the banks' USD denominated offshore remittance flows. The deal was placed with Japanese institutional investors, who required hedging on the currency mismatch. To reduce the credit exposure for the institution providing the currency swap, the issue obtained a PSG from the IFC. This instrument has not yet been used for green projects in Thailand
First-loss provisions	First-loss provisions refer to any device designed to protect investors from the loss of capital that is exposed first if there is a financial loss of security. These could be debt, equity, or derivatives instruments including mezzanine finance, cash facilities, or guarantees. They could also take the form of insurance that insures debt security providers who are liable to pay compensation to the investors, irrespective of the cause of the loss.	The Green Cornerstone Bond Fund, created by the IFC and Amundi and launched in March 2018, is the world's largest targeted green bond fund focused on investing in emerging markets. To lower risk and attract private investments, the IFC will provide a first-loss coverage through a junior tranche. The Credit Guarantee Investment Facility provides credit guarantees for local currency denominated bonds issued by investment grade companies in ASEAN+3 countries. This instrument has not yet been used for green projects in Thailand
Contingent loans	Contingent loans are often used in project finance to backstop the main debt by providing a payment option for specific case scenarios. For instance, if the government fails to obtain quality cash flows, the contingent loan is triggered, and investors are paid.	There have been no green projects using contingent loans. This instrument has not yet been used for green projects in Thailand

(continued)

Credit enhancement mechanisms	Definition	Example
Concessional loan	Concessional loans are loans that are granted on substantially more generous terms compared to market loans, which are achieved through below-the-market interest rates, longer grant periods, or a combination of both.	The Thailand Refrigeration and Air Conditioning (RAC) NAMA Support Project is designed to support energy savings and climate change targets in Thailand through the utilization of climate-friendly and energy-efficient cooling technologies. Part of the financial support from the project is a grant or soft loan for producers switching to natural refrigerant products. The project also offers zero or low interest rates to product dealers and financial institutions.[362]
ESCOs	Energy Service Companies (ESCOs) provide technical and financial services for the implementation of energy efficiency solutions. Under a Guaranteed Saving Schemes, the ESCO guarantees a certain level of energy savings, thus assuming the performance risk. With a Shared Savings Model, higher energy savings determine a lower cost of the energy service. In both schemes, financing can come either from the ESCO or a third party.	ESCOs are quite common in Thailand. The companies were gathered and formed the Thai ESCO Association which plays a central role in conducting EE projects in Thailand. The Thailand ESCO pilot project is Gas Turbine Generator (GTG) Cogeneration Power Plant of Bangkok Produce Merchandising Public Co., Ltd in Saraburi.[363]
Viability gap funding (VGF)	VGF is used specifically in infrastructure to cover for the heavy upfront funding that is required to kick start projects. An analysis of the viability of a proposed project points out the weak areas that prevent large-scale funding from being obtained. A VGF scheme can be implemented through capital grants, subordinated loans, or even interest subsidies to target issues that are affecting the viability of the project. A blended finance approach could also be used to reduce project risk.	Malaysia has established the Facilitation Fund from the national budget. The fund is used to help bridge the viability gaps of PPP projects in Malaysia.[364] This instrument has not yet been used in Thailand.[365]
A/B loans or grants	A/B loans or grants are where a Multilateral Development Bank (MDB) offers the "A" portion of the loan while attracting other lenders to join in a second (or "B") tranche. The MDB will be the lender-of-record, lead lender, and administrative agent in the transaction. This reduces part of the risks of the operations, by also being covered by the "umbrella" of the MDBs that includes a preferred creditor status and de jure immunity from taxation.	Italian transmissions system operator Terna issued a USD81 million green loan in project finance format in July 2017. The Inter-American Development Bank offered the USD56 million A loan and BBVA subscribed a B loan for USD25 million. The deal will finance the design and construction of a 213 km transmission line of 500 kilovolts in the northeast of Uruguay In 2021, ADB supports A/B loans for a Green Yellow Rooftop Solar in Thailand. The project entails 92 solar photovoltaic systems located on the premises of large commercial and industrial consumers throughout Thailand, with a total installed capacity of 60.3 MW.[366]

Annex IV. Risk transfer and/or risk sharing mechanisms

Risk transfer instruments	Definition	Example
First-loss capital	May provide a risk buffer for green structures and thereby encourage institutional investors. First loss capital is incorporated into the capital structure usually as a junior equity tranche or as subordinated debt.	The AUD100 million equity investment by the Clean Energy Finance Corporation (CEFC) in Australian Prime Property Fund Commercial. This instrument has not yet been used for green projects in Thailand
Synthetic green capital notes or securitisation	Risk management (de-risking) to release loss reserves, with the use of freed capital to fund green projects. Reduce risk weighting of assets, while keeping the assets tied to the banks' balance sheet and the current operations.	A global example is the USD3 billion synthetic ABS by Credit Agricole used to free up risk capital for green loan origination. This instrument has not yet been used for green projects in Thailand
Loan loss reserves	Pooled public funds are set aside by a financial institution to partially recover loss in their loan portfolio in case of borrower defaults. If the institution issues green bonds, loan loss reserves can improve the risk profile of the deal by providing additional assurance on issuer cash flows.	This instrument has not yet been used for green projects in Thailand
Risk sharing facility (RSF)/ Default swap	These structures support a transaction involving a loss-sharing agreement, where the originator will be reimbursed in the case of a loss of principal on a portfolio of eligible assets (mortgages, consumer or student debt, energy efficiency loans, SME loans, receivables). Originators are mainly banks and corporations.	This instrument has not yet been used for green projects in Thailand

Annex V. Examples of Green standards applicable in Thailand

Green Standard	Description	Sectors	Applicability in Thailand
National			
Green building energy code (GBEC)[367]	Issued by the Ministry of Energy under Section 19 of the Energy Conservation Promotion Act, the green building energy code (GBEC) lays down certain standards and specifications that building design and construction must adhere to (i) its building envelope, (ii) electrical lighting system, (iii) air conditioning system, (iv) water heating, (v) overall energy consumption, and (vi) renewable energy outfitting within the building. The code became binding on state agency buildings in 2013 and presents the first compulsory energy consumption standards to have universal application in Thailand.	Buildings, Energy Efficiency	This code applies to nine types of new buildings, including hotels, condominiums, hospitals, education institutions, theatres, entertainment centres, offices, department stores, and convention halls. The enforcement starts with new or retrofitted buildings being constructed which have a total area of all stories equal to 2000 m² or more.[368, 369]
Rating of Energy and Environmental Sustainability (TREES)[370,371,372,373]	The Rating of Energy and Environmental Sustainability of Thailand was introduced by the Thai Green Building Institute in 2008. It is voluntary and applicable to green buildings in Thailand. The criteria are based on (i) Building Management, (ii) Site and Landscape, (iii) Water Conservation, (iv) Energy and Atmosphere, (v) Materials and Resources, (vi) Environmental Protection, and (vii) Green Innovation.[374] The energy efficiency section is referenced to the Ministerial Regulation Prescribing the Type or Size of Building and Standards, Criteria and Procedures for Designing Buildings for Energy Conservation, BE 2552.	Buildings	The rating system is divided into four categories: (i) TREES-NC for certifying new and major renovated projects, (ii) TREES-Pre-NC for new or major renovated projects in the design phase, (iii) TREES-EB for existing building projects, and (iv) TREES-CS for building structure, envelope and Heating Ventilation and Air-Conditioning system of new or major renovated projects. As of August 2021, there have been 72 projects being awarded TREES certification.[375]
Thailand Energy and Environmental Assessment Method (TEEAM)[376]	The Thailand Energy and Environmental Assessment Method (TEEAM) is introduced by the Ministry of Energy as a green building rating system based on Thai building energy code BE 2552. It was developed based on reviewing labelling schemes from other countries as well as Thailand standards and codes of practice. There are 9 items to be assessed, including (i) site location, (ii) layout and landscape, (iii) building envelope, (iv) HVAC system, (v) lighting system, (vi) passive and renewable energy and energy management, (vii) sanitary system, (viii) materials and method of construction, and (ix) design and energy conservation strategies.[377]	Buildings	The method applies to residential and non-residential buildings: offices, hospitals, hotels, and department stores.
Thai Green Label Scheme (GL)[378]	The Thai Green Label was developed by the Ministry of Industry and launched by the Thailand Environmental Institute (TEI) in 1994 as an environmental certification awarded to products with minimum detrimental impacts to the environment. It is a voluntary scheme and emphasises natural resources conservation, pollution reduction, and waste management.[379]	Industry, products	As of July 2021, The Thai Green Label has been developed for 127 products, which also covers construction products such as insulation material, paint, and tiles.[380]
EGAT Label No. 5	The Label No. 5 standard defines the energy performance of relevant building systems.	Residential buildings	The EGAT Label No. 5 standard is known and used locally.

(continued)

Green Standard	Description	Sectors	Applicability in Thailand
National			
ECO Village Standard[381]	The ECO Village building standard, which was conceived by NHA as a standard for sustainable housing and urban community development, was designed for NHA by the Faculty of Architecture of Chulalongkorn University. The standard was based on a review of international green standards such as LEED, BREEAM, and GASBEE. Elements of these standards were adapted for application in Thailand, with an emphasis on their applicability for low-income housing developments. The ECO Village standard provides guidelines and standards for the design and construction of environmentally friendly housing project developments. The ECO building standard Village standard takes a more holistic approach to the environmental performance of a building and addresses other sustainability issues. It is a comprehensive standard, covering issues 6 such as site location, energy and water savings, building materials, and indoor air quality. NHA uses the ECO Village standard as a tool for the design and construction of sustainable housing and urban community developments, with the aim to achieve the UN Sustainable Development Goals (including SDGs 3, 7, 10, 11, and 12).	Low-income housing	The standard is only known and used locally.
Regional			
ASEAN Green Bond Standards (AGBS)[382]	The standards were developed and launched in November 2017 by the ASEAN Capital Markets Forum. The standards also guide the classification of green projects in the region that qualify for the AGBS label in the region. These projects specifically exclude fossil fuel-related projects. Companies in Malaysia, Singapore, and Indonesia have already issued bonds labelled as ASEAN Green Bonds. [383]	Energy, Transport, Water, Buildings, ICT, Waste, Nature Based Assets, Industry and Commercial activities.	The standards can be applied in Thailand.[384]
ASEAN Sustainability Bond Standards (ASEAN SUS)[385]	The standards provide the framework to finance or re-finance a combination of both Green and Social Projects that respectively offer environmental and social benefits. It They also provides guidance onguide the classification of sustainable projects.	Energy, Transport, Water, Buildings, ICT, Waste, Nature Based Assets, Industry and Commercial activities.	The standards can be applied in Thailand.[386]
Global			
National Standards for Environmental Management Systems (ISO 14001)[387]	The ISO 14001 standard specifies requirements for an effective environmental management system (EMS). It provides a framework that an organization can follow to better control its environmental impacts.	Waste, commercial activities	The standard can be applied in Thailand.[388]
Effective energy management systems (EnMS)/ ISO 50001[389]	The ISO 50001 standard establishes an international framework for the supply, use, and consumption of energy in industrial, commercial, and institutional organizations. Implement an ISO 50001 compliant sustainable energy management system and demonstrate organiszational's commitment to continuously improving energy performance, leading to economic benefits and reduced greenhouse gas emissions.	Renewable energy, Energy efficiency	The standard can be applied in Thailand.[390]

(continued)

Green Standard	Description	Sectors	Applicability in Thailand
National			
Climate Bonds Taxonomy and Standard[391]	Climate Bonds Taxonomy is used to identify green projects and assets which are aligned with achieving the goals of the Paris Agreement. This excludes assets such as fossil fuel power generation, internal combustion engine personal vehicles and new roads and infrastructure that facilitate their movement, and freight rail and shipping for fossil fuel transportation. The Climate Bonds Standard includes detailed and science-based sector-specific criteria and other process rules for green bonds, against which an issuer can seek Climate Bonds Certification for an individual debt instrument of issuance prorgamme. The Certification process is facilitated by a third-party Approved Verifier and is awarded by the Climate Bonds Standards Board.	Energy, Transport, Water, Buildings, ICT, Waste, Nature Based Assets, Industry and Commercial activities.	The taxonomy can be applied in any jurisdiction, including Thailand. As of November 2021, nine Thai green bonds had been Certified against the Climate Bonds Standard, and several more issued in alignment with the Climate Bonds Taxonomy.[392]
SOURCE	SOURCE is a global standard created by Sustainable Infrastructure Foundation (SIF). It offers governments a global, reliable, secure, and user-friendly project preparation software to maximize public sector users financing options including PPPs by providing well-prepared projects consistently and transparently to the international community of contractors, investors, and lenders.	Infrastructure	This standard can be applied in Thailand
The Standard for Sustainable and Resilient Infrastructure (SuRe)	SuRe is a global voluntary standard that integrates key criteria of sustainability and resilience into infrastructure development and upgrades, through 14 themes covering 61 criteria across governance, social and environmental factors.	Infrastructure	The standards can be applied in Thailand.
Envision	Envision is a framework that includes 64 sustainability and resilience indicators, called 'credits', organized around five categories: Quality of Life, Leadership, Resource Allocation, Natural World, and Climate and Resilience. These collectively address areas of human wellbeing, mobility, community development, collaboration, planning, economy, materials, energy, water, sitting, conservation, ecology, emissions, and resilience.	Infrastructure	The standards can be applied in Thailand.
LEED (Leadership in Energy and Environmental Design)	LEED is the most widely used green building rating system in the world. Available for virtually all building types, LEED provides a framework for healthy, highly efficient, and cost-saving green buildings.[393]	Buildings	The standard can be applied in Thailand.

Annex VI. A Sample Pipeline of Green Infrastructure Projects

The sample pipeline consists of a list of green and potentially green projects in the seven sectors: low carbon and/or sustainable transport, renewable energy, sustainable water management, sustainable waste management, building, smart cities, and coastal zone management. The greenness selection criteria are based on the Climate Bonds Taxonomy as introduced in Section 3. The sample green project pipeline comprises three categories of project status: planned, under construction, and completed. The planned and under construction categories aim to introduce current and future investment opportunities for green infrastructure in Thailand. The completed projects, which are high-profile, are included for demonstration purposes but also considering the refinancing potential in the context of Thailand.

Project Name	Location	Cost	Status	Greenness	Pipeline source
TRANSPORT					
Chiang Mai Mass Transit, Red line Project (2020–2027)[394]	Chiang Mai Province, Thailand	THB27.2 bn (USD827m)	Planned	Green	PPP Plan 2020–2027
Nakhon Ratchasima Mass Transit Project (Green Line) (2020–2027)[395, 396]	Nakhon Ratchasima Province, Thailand	THB 7.1 bn (USD217.4m)	Planned	Green	PPP Plan 2020–2027
Phuket Mass Transit Project (2020–2027)[397, 398]	Phuket Province	THB35.3 bn (USD1.07bn)	Planned	Green	PPP Plan 2020–2027
Khon Kaen Mass Transit Project (2020–2027)[399, 400]	Khon Kaen Province	THB22 bn (USD686.6m)	Planned	Green	PPP Plan 2020–2027
Enhancement of Private Sector Participation in Freight Transportation by Rail Project (2020–2027)[401, 402]	Nong Khai–Laem Chabang route	THB25.9 bn (USD788m)	Planned	Green	PPP Plan 2020–2027
Bangkok–Nakhon Ratchasima High Speed Rail Project, 2020[403]	Bangkok–Nakhon Ratchasima Province	THB179.4 bn (USD5.73bn)	Completed	Green	SRT, BoI
Mass Rapid Transit Pink Line Project, BTS Group Holdings Public Company Limited, under the consortium Northern Bangkok Monorail Company Limited, 2017.[404]	Bangkok	THB56.7 bn (USD1.7bn)	Under construction	Green	Mass Rapid Transit Authority (MRTA)
Mass Rapid Transit Yellow Line Project, BTS Group Holdings Public Company Limited, under the consortium Eastern Bangkok Monorail Company Limited, 2017[405]	Bangkok	THB54.8 bn (USD1.656bn)	Under construction	Green	MRTA
Mass Rapid Transit Orange East Line, Mass Rapid Transit Authority of Thailand (SOE)[406]	Bangkok	THB113.3 bn (USD3.78bn)	Under construction	Green	MRTA
Mass Rapid Transit Orange East Line, Mass Rapid Transit Authority of Thailand (SOE)[407]	Bangkok	THB258 bn (USD7.84bn)	Under construction	Green	SRT
Mass Rapid Transit Orange East Line, Mass Rapid Transit Authority of Thailand (SOE)[408]	Bangkok	THB124.79bn (USD3.79bn)	Planned	Green	MRTA
SOLAR					
73 MW Lopburi Solar Farm, Natural Energy Development, Electricity Generating Public Company Limited, 2012[409]	Lopburi Province	USD250m	Completed	Green	ADB

(continued)

Project Name	Location	Cost	Status	Greenness	Pipeline source
WIND					
10 MW Southern Thailand Wind Power and Battery Energy Storage Project, BCPG Public Company Limited (BCPG), 2020[410]	Nakhon Sithammarat Province	THB825m (USD27 million)	Completed	Green	BCPG
90 MW Subyai Wind Power Project, Electricity Generating Public Company Limited, 2016[411]	Chaiyaphum Province	USD200m	Completed	Green	ADB
260 MW Hanuman Wind Farm Project, Energy Absolute Public Company Limited, 2019[412, 413]	Chaiyaphum Province	THB20bn (USD645m)	Completed	Green	ADB, Energy Absolute PCL
BIOMASS					
25 MW Gulf Chana Green Biomass Project, Chana Green Company Limited, 2020[414, 415]	Chana, Songkhla Province	THB2.3bn (USD73.5m)	Completed	Green	ADB, GULF
9.9 MW Khlong Khlung Biomass Power Plant, Absolute Clean Energy Public Company Limited, 2021[416]	Kampangphet Province	THB1.059 bn (USD33.78m)	Under construction	Green	Absolute Clean Energy PLC
23 MW Biomass Power Project, Absolute Clean Energy Public Company Limited, 2023[417]	Ranong Province	THB 981.50m (USD29.8m)	Planned	Green	Absolute Clean Energy PLC
9.9 MW Biomass Power Project, Absolute Clean Energy Public Company Limited, 2022[418]	Supanburi Province	THB820m (USD24.9m)	Planned	Green	Absolute Clean Energy PLC
9.9 MW Biomass Power Project, Absolute Clean Energy Public Company Limited, 2022[419]	Nakornpathom Province	THB820m (USD24.9m)	Planned	Green	Absolute Clean Energy PLC
9.9 MW Biomass Power Project, Absolute Clean Energy Public Company Limited, 2022[420]	Nakhon Ratchasima	THB820m (USD24.9m)	Planned	Green	Absolute Clean Energy PLC
HYBRID (Solar–Hydro)					
2,725 MW 16 Hydro–Floating Solar Hybrid Projects, Electricity Generating Authority of Thailand (EGAT), 2021–2027[421, 422]	Ubon Ratchathani, Tak, Khon Kaen, Kanchanaburi, Chaiyaphum, Yala, Surat Thani. Uttaradit Provinces	THB 2.3 bn (USD68.8m)	Planned	Green	EGAT

(continued)

Project Name	Location	Cost	Status	Greenness	Pipeline source
WASTE					
9.8 MW Waste to Energy Project, Global Power Synergy PCL (GPSC) 2019[423, 424]	Amphur Mueang, Rayong Province	THB1.6 bn (USD51.36m)	Completed	Green	GPSC
Integrated Waste Management Project, Global Power Synergy PCL (GPSC) and Rayong PAO, 2018[425]	Rayong Province	THB600m (USD18.6m)	Completed	Green	GPSC
Waste Management Project, PJT Technology Co., Ltd (Thailand) and Phuket City Municipality, 2012[426]	Phuket Province	THB940m (USD30.3m)	THB940m	Completed	Institute for Global Environmental Strategies (IGES)
SUEZ Plastic Recycling Plant, 2020[427]	Bang Phli District, Bangkok	N/A	Completed	Green	SUEZ
Chonburi Clean Energy Plant (CCE), 2019[428]	Eastern Economic Corridor (EEC) zone, Chonburi	USD59.3m.	Completed	Green	SUEZ, CCE
A fully integrated biopolymer production facility, GC International Corporation Company Limited and Cargill Incorporated, 2021[429]	Nakhon Sawan Province	THB20bn (USD607.9m)	Planned	Green	PTT Global Chemical PCL
WATER					
Thai Tap Water (TTW) Water Production and Distribution Concession Project, 2005[430]	Nakhon Pathom and Samut Sakhon Provinces, Thailand	USD235m	Completed	Green	World Bank Private Participation in Infrastructure (PPI) project
Lam Nam Chi Reservoir Project, Royal Irrigation Department (RID), 2019[431]	Chaiyaphum Province	THB3.1bn (USD100m)	Under construction	Potentially Green	The Royal Irrigation Department, Ministry of Agriculture and Cooperatives
Khlong Toei Wastewater Treatment Facility, BMA, (2020–2027)[432]	Bangkok	THB12.47bn (USD379m)	Planned	Green	PPP Plan 2020–2027
Construction of the CLS Dam Project and wastewater collection system at Saen Saeb Canal, BMA, (2022–2026)[433, 434]	Bangkok	THB1.8 bn (USD54.68m)	Planned	Potentially Green	BMA
Construction of a drainage tunnel for the Phraya Ratchamontri canal From Phasicharoen Canal to Sanam Chai Canal, BMA, (2022–2026)[435, 436]	Bangkok	THB6.13 bn (USD186m)	Planned	Potentially Green	BMA

(continued)

Project Name	Location	Cost	Status	Greenness	Pipeline source
WATER					
Construction of the CSL Dam, Khlong Bangna from Praap Khlong Kled to the Chao Phraya River area, BMA (2022–2025)[437]	Bangkok	THB1.98 bn (USD60.2m)	Planned	Green	BMA
Nong Bon Swamp Wastewater Treatment Facility, BMA (2020– 2027)[438]	Bangkok	THB7.9 bn (USD240.8m)	Planned	Green	PPP Plan 2020–2027
Don Mueang Wastewater Treatment Facility, BMA (2020–2027)[439,440]	Bangkok	THB5.9 bn (USD179.3m)	Planned	Green	PPP Plan 2020–2027
Bang Khen Wastewater Treatment Facility, BMA (2020–2027)[441,442]	Bangkok	THB7.25 bn (USD220.3m)	Planned	Green	PPP Plan 2020–2027

Endnotes

1. Climate Bonds Initiative. 2019. Green Infrastructure Investment Opportunities (GIIO) Programme. https://www.climatebonds.net/green-infrastructure-investment-opportunities-giio-programme
2. Stock Exchange of Thailand (SET). 2020. Thai listed companies mark ASEAN's top inclusions in Dow Jones Sustainability World Index (DJSI World). Retrieved from https://www.set.or.th/set/pdfnews.do?newsId=16054795884190&sequence=0
3. World Bank. 2021. Country Overview, Thailand. Retrieved from www.worldbank.org/en/country/thailand/overview
4. Asian Development Bank (ADB). 2021. Asian Development Outlook 2021 Update, Transforming Agriculture in Asia. Retrieved from https://www.adb.org/sites/default/files/publication/726556/ado2021-update.pdf
5. World Bank and ADB. 2021. Climate Risk Country Profile: Thailand. Retrieved from https://reliefweb.int/sites/reliefweb.int/files/resources/climate-risk-country-profile-thailand.pdf
6. World Bank. 2012. Thai Flood 2011. Retrieved from https://documents1.worldbank.org/curated/en/677841468335414861/pdf/698220WP0v10P106011020120Box370022B.pdf
7. World Bank, 2011, The World Bank Supports Thailand's Post-Floods Recovery Effort. Retrieved from https://www.worldbank.org/en/news/feature/2011/12/13/world-bank-supports-thailands-post-floods-recovery-effort
8. Germanwatch. 2019. Global Climate Risk Index 2020. Retrieved from https://germanwatch.org/sites/default/files/20-2-01e%20Global%20Climate%20Risk%20Index%202020_14.pdf
9. World Bank and ADB. 2021. Climate Risk Country Profile: Thailand. Retrieved from https://reliefweb.int/sites/reliefweb.int/files/resources/climate-risk-country-profile-thailand.pdf
10. Office of Natural Resources and Environmental Policy and Planning (ONEP), Ministry of Natural Resources and Environmental (MNRE). 2015. Thailand's Intended Nationally Determined Contribution (INDC). Retrieved from https://www4.unfccc.int/sites/ndcstaging/PublishedDocuments/Thailand%20First/Thailand_INDC.pdf
11. Bangkok Post. 2021. Carbon neutrality by 2065. Retrieved from https://www.bangkokpost.com/thailand/general/2196471/carbon-neutrality-by-2065-vows-pm
12. International Energy Agency (IEA), 2020. Putting a price on carbon – an efficient way for Thailand to meet its bold emission target. Retrieved from https://www.iea.org/articles/putting-a-price-on-carbon-an-efficient-way-for-thailand-to-meet-its-bold-emission-target
13. Ibid.
14. World Bank. 2021, Country Overview. Retrieved from https://www.worldbank.org/en/country/thailand/overview#1
15. ADB. 2021. Asian Development Outlook 2021 Update Transforming Agriculture in Asia. Retrieved from https://www.adb.org/sites/default/files/publication/726556/ado2021-update.pdf
16. World Bank. 2021. Thailand Economic Monitor July 2021. Retrieved from https://www.worldbank.org/en/country/thailand/publication/thailand-economic-monitor-july-2021-the-road-to-recovery
17. ADB. 2021. Implementing a Green Recovery in Southeast Asia. Retrieved from https://www.adb.org/sites/default/files/publication/684966/adb-brief-173-green-recovery-southeast-asia.pdf
18. Organisation for Economic Co-operation and Development (OECD). 2021. Investment Policy Reviews: Thailand. Retrieved from https://www.oecd-ilibrary.org/sites/6091762f-en/index.html?itemId=/content/component/6091762f-en
19. Price Waterhouse Coopers (PWC). 2021. Thailand's Infrastructure Market Update and Outlook. Retrieved from https://www.pwc.com/th/en/deals/capital-projects-n-infrastructure/thailand-infrastructure-market-update-and-outlook.html
20. Ibid.
21. Interview with representatives from the BTS Group. October 15, 2020.
22. Office of the National Economic and Social Development Council (NESDC), Thailand. 2019. National Strategy (2018-2037). Retrieved from http://nscr.nesdb.go.th/wp-content/uploads/2019/10/National-Strategy-Eng-Final-25-OCT-2019.pdf
23. NESDC. 2021. Draft Thirteenth National Economic and Social Development Plan (2023–2027) (For public consultation). Retrieved from https://www.nesdc.go.th/download/document/Yearend/2021/plan13.pdf
24. ADB. 2020. ADB Supports Thailand's Green, Social, and Sustainability Bonds for COVID-19 Recovery. Retrieved from https://www.adb.org/news/adb-supports-thailand-green-social-and-sustainability-bonds-covid-19-recovery
25. Climate Bonds Initiative (CBI), 2020. Thai Govt Marks 2020 with Certified Sovereign Green Issuance: Commitment to Recovery, Sustainability, Infrastructure. Retrieved from https://www.climatebonds.net/2020/12/thai-govt-marks-2020-certified-sovereign-green-issuance-commitment-recovery-sustainability
26. Public Debt Management Office (PDMO), Ministry of Finance (MOF), Thailand. 2021. 2020 Sustainability Bond Interim Report A Year of Accomplishments. Retrieved from https://www.pdmo.go.th/pdmomedia/documents/2021/Feb/Minister%20Approved%202020.pdf
27. PDMO, MOF, Thailand. 2020. The 2nd successful tranche of sustainability bond reaffirms the Thai Government's commitment to the UN Sustainable Development Goals (SDGs). Retrieved from https://www.pdmo.go.th/pdmomedia/documents/2020/Nov/%E0%B9%81%E0%B8%96%E0%B8%A5%E0%B8%87%E0%B8%82%E0%B9%88%E0%B8%B2%E0%B8%A7%20ESGLB35DA%20%E0%B8%84%E0%B8%A3%E0%B8%B1%E0%B9%89%E0%B8%87%E0%B8%97-%E0%B8%B5%E0%B9%88%201_2564%201.1.docx.pdf
28. CBI. 2020. "Thai Govt Marks 2020 with Certified Sovereign Green Issuance: Commitment to Recovery, Sustainability, Infrastructure." Retrieved from https://www.climatebonds.net/2020/12/thai-govt-marks-2020-certified-sovereign-green-issuance-commitment-recovery-sustainability
29. Fiscal Policy Office (FPO), the Bank of Thailand (BOT), the Securities and Exchange Commission (SEC), the Office of Insurance Commission (OIC), and the Stock Exchange of Thailand (SET). 2021. Sustainable Finance Initiatives for Thailand. Retrieved from https://www.bot.or.th/Thai/SustainableBanking/Documents/Sustainable_Finance_Initiatives_for_Thailand.pdf
30. Ibid.
31. Worldometers. 2021. Thailand Population. Retrieved from https://www.worldometers.info/world-population/thailand-Retrieved from population/#:~:text=The%20current%20population%20of%20Thailand,the%20latest%20United%20Nations%20data.
32. Macrotrends. 2021. Thailand Population Growth Rate. Retrieved from https://www.macrotrends.net/countries/THA/thailand/population-growth-rate
33. Knoema. 2020. Thailand-Urban Population as a Share of Total Population. Retrieved from https://knoema.com/atlas/Thailand/Urban-population#:~:text=In%202020%2C%20urban%20population%20for,defined%20by%20national%20statistical%20offices.
34. World Bank. 2020. Thailand GDP Data. Retrieved from https://data.worldbank.org/indicator/NY.GDP.MKTP.CD?locations=TH
35. ADB. 2021. Asian Development Outlook 2021 Update, Transforming Agriculture in Asia. Retrieved from https://www.adb.org/sites/default/files/publication/726556/ado2021-update.pdf
36. CEIC Data, 2021, Thailand Policy Rate. Retrieved from https://www.ceicdata.com/en/indicator/thailand/policy-rate
37. Focuseconomics. 2021. Thailand Inflation. Retrieved from https://www.focus-economics.com/countries/thailand/news/inflation/inflation-hits-highest-level-since-december-2012-in-april
38. World Bank. 2019. Foreign Direct Investment Data in Thailand. Retrieved from https://data.worldbank.org/indicator/BX.KLT.DINV.CD.WD?locations=TH
39. Statista,.2021. FDI Net Inflows in Thailand from 2013–2020. Retrieved from https://www.statista.com/statistics/607941/thailand-foreign-direct-investment-net-inflows/
40. Trading Economics. 2021. Thailand Government Bond 10Y. Retrieved from https://tradingeconomics.com/thailand/government-bond-yield
41. CEIC Data, 2021, Thailand Trade Balance. Retrieved from https://www.ceicdata.com/en/indicator/thailand/trade-balance
42. Countryeconomy. 2021. Thailand National Debt. Retrieved from https://countryeconomy.com/national-debt/thailand
43. Countryeconomy, 2021, Thailand Credit Rating. Retrieved from https://countryeconomy.com/ratings/thailand
44. ADB. 2021. Thailand: Country Partnership Strategy (2021–2025). Retrieved from https://www.adb.org/documents/thailand-country-partnership-strategy-2021-2025
45. World Bank. 2021. Country Overview, Thailand. Retrieved from https://www.worldbank.org/en/country/thailand/overview#1
46. ADB. 2021. Thailand: Country Partnership Strategy (2021–2025). Retrieved from https://www.adb.org/documents/thailand-country-partnership-strategy-2021-2025
47. World Bank. 2021. Country Overview, Thailand. Retrieved from https://www.worldbank.org/en/country/thailand/overview#1
48. ADB. 2021. Thailand: Country Partnership Strategy (2021–2025). Retrieved from https://www.adb.org/documents/thailand-country-partnership-strategy-2021-2025
49. ADB. 2021. Thailand: Country Partnership Strategy (2021–2025). Retrieved from https://www.adb.org/documents/thailand-country-partnership-strategy-2021-2025
50. ADB. 2021. Thailand: Country Partnership Strategy (2021–2025). Retrieved from https://www.adb.org/documents/thailand-country-partnership-strategy-2021-2025
51. International Monetary Fund (IMF). 2021. Country Report No, 21/97, Thailand. Statement by Ms. Alisara Mahasandana, Executive Director for Thailand and Mr. Krist Dacharux, Advisor to Executive Director May 17, 2021. Retrieved from https://www.imf.org/en/Publications/CR/Issues/2021/06/02/Thailand-2021-Article-IV-Consultation-Press-Release-Staff-Report-and-Statement-by-the-50192
52. Board of Investment (BOI), Thailand. 2021. Thailand Economic Outlook and Key Economic Policies. Retrieved from https://www.boi.go.th/upload/content/Thailand%20Economic%20Outlook%202021%20EN_6034b4cfeaaf8.pdf
53. World Bank. 2021. Country Overview, Thailand. Retrieved from https://www.worldbank.org/en/country/thailand/overview#1
54. Tradingeconomics. 2021. Thailand Unemployment Rate. Retrieved from https://tradingeconomics.com/thailand/unemployment-rate
55. Bank of Thailand (BOT). Database on loans to households. Retrieved from https://www.bot.or.th/App/BTWS_STAT/statistics/BOTWEBSTAT.aspx?reportID=775&language=eng
56. International Monetary Fund (IMF). 2021. Country Report No, 21/97, Thailand. Appendix V. Retrieved from https://www.imf.org/en/Publications/CR/Issues/2021/06/02/Thailand-2021-Article-IV-Consultation-Press-Release-Staff-Report-and-Statement-by-the-50192
57. World Bank. 2021. Thailand Economic Monitor July 2021. Retrieved from https://www.worldbank.org/en/country/thailand/publication/thailand-economic-monitor-july-2021-the-road-to-recovery
58. BOI. 2021. Thailand Economic Outlook and Key Economic Policies. Retrieved from https://www.boi.go.th/upload/content/Thailand%20Economic%20Outlook%202021%20EN_6034b4cfeaaf8.pdf
59. Countryeconomy, 2021, Thailand National Debt. Retrieved from https://countryeconomy.com/national-debt/thailand
60. IMF. 2021. Country Report No, 21/97, Thailand, Appendix VI. Retrieved from https://www.imf.org/en/Publications/CR/Issues/2021/06/02/Thailand-2021-Article-IV-Consultation-Press-Release-Staff-Report-and-Statement-by-the-50192
61. Moody's Investor Service, 2020. Retrieved from https://www.moodys.com/research/Moodys-affirms-ThaiBevs-Baa3-rating-changes-outlook-to-stable--PR_437101
62. Bangkok Post, 2021, June Exports at 11 Year High as Global Demand Rebounds. Retrieved from https://www.bangkokpost.com/business/2153731/june-exports-at-11-year-high-as-global-demand-rebounds
63. BOT. Database on rates of Exchange of Commercial Banks in Bangkok Metropolis (2002-present). Retrieved from https://www.bot.or.th/App/BTWS_STAT/statistics/ReportPage.aspx?reportID=123&language=eng
64. Bangkok Post. 2021. Government to Raise Debt Ceiling. Retrieved from https://www.bangkokpost.com/thailand/general/2184923/govt-to-raise-debt-ceiling
65. CEIC Data. 2021. Thailand Policy Rate. Retrieved from https://www.ceicdata.com/en/indicator/thailand/policy-rate
66. IMF. 2021, Policy Responses to COVID-19. Retrieved from https://www.imf.org/en/Topics/imf-and-covid19/Policy-Responses-to-COVID-19#T
67. BOT. 2021. Thailand Monetary Policy. Retrieved from https://www.bot.or.th/English/MonetaryPolicy/MonetPolicyKnowledge/pages/target.aspx
68. Asian Development Bank (ADB). 2021. Asian Development Outlook 2021 Update, Transforming Agriculture in Asia. Retrieved from https://www.adb.org/sites/default/files/publication/726556/ado2021-update.pdf
69. World Bank. 2021. Thailand Economic Monitor July 2021. Retrieved from https://www.worldbank.org/en/country/thailand/publication/thailand-economic-monitor-july-2021-the-road-to-recovery
70. PWC. 2021. Thailand's Infrastructure Market Update and Outlook. Retrieved from https://www.pwc.com/th/en/deals/capital-projects-n-infrastructure/thailand-infrastructure-market-update-and-outlook.html
71. BOI. 2015, Enhancing Infrastructure Development for Thailand's Future Growth. Retrieved from https://www.boi.go.th/upload/content/5.%20Enhancing%20Infrastructure%20Development%20f_92919.pdf
72. Oxford Business Group. 2017. Thailand Transport. Retrieved from https://oxfordbusinessgroup.com/overview/path-prosperity-infrastructure-improvements-are-heart-plans-connect-thailand-rest-asia-0
73. PWC. 2021. Thailand's Infrastructure Market Update and Outlook. Retrieved from https://www.pwc.com/th/en/deals/capital-projects-n-infrastructure/thailand-infrastructure-market-update-and-outlook.html
74. Dezan Shira & Associates ASEAN Briefing.2018. Thailand's Eastern Economic Corridor. Retrieved from https://www.aseanbriefing.com/news/thailand-eastern-economic-corridor/
75. PWC. 2021. Thailand's Infrastructure Market Update and Outlook. Retrieved from https://www.pwc.com/th/en/deals/capital-projects-n-infrastructure/thailand-infrastructure-market-update-and-outlook.html
76. Ibid.
77. The Nation. 2020. Southern Economic Corridor. Retrieved from https://www.nationthailand.com/in-focus/30395128
78. PWC. 2021. Thailand's Infrastructure Market Update and Outlook. Retrieved from https://www.pwc.com/th/en/deals/capital-projects-n-infrastructure/thailand-infrastructure-market-update-and-outlook.htmll
79. Ibid.
80. United Nations Economic and Social Commission for Asia and the Pacific (UNESCAP), Public and Private Partnership (PPP) in Thailand. Retrieved from https://www.unescap.org/sites/default/files/Rules%20and%20Regulations_Public%20Private%20Partnership_Thailand.pdf
81. Sitthiyot, Thitithep. 2017. "The Truth about Thailand's Transport Infrastructure Development and Financing" Nomura Journal Of Asian Capital Markets. Spring 2017 Vol.1/No.2, pp.38-43. Retrieved from https://www.nomurafoundation.or.jp/wordpress/wp-content/uploads/2017/04/NJACM1-1SP17-08.pdf

82. State Enterprise Policy Office (SEPO). 2018. "The Launch of Thailand Future Fund", a presentation by Prapas Kong-Ied, Director-General of SEPO, given at "Thailand Focus 2018: The Future is Now" 29th August 2018, Grand Hyatt Erawan Bangkok Hotel. Retrieved from http://www.sepo.go.th/assets/document/file/Thailand%20Focus%202018%20v20-8-2018%20editted.pdf

83. Mahanakorn Partners Group. 2021. Capital Projects & Infrastructure, 2021. Retrieved from https://www.linkedin.com/pulse/capital-projects-infrastructure-thailand-luca-bernardinetti/

84. SEPO. 2020. Public-Private Partnership Project Delivery Plan 2020 – 2027. Retrieved from http://www.ppp.sepo.go.th/tinymce/plugins/filemanager/thumbs/PPP%20Delivery%20Plan%202020-2027_Mar2020%20(EN).pdf

85. SEPO. 2019. Public-Private Partnership (PPP) Act, B.E. 2562 (2019). Retrieved from http://www.ppp.sepo.go.th/tinymce/plugins/filemanager/thumbs/PPP-ACT-2-9-62-v1-1.pdf

86. ADB. 2020. Green Finance Strategies for Post-COVID-19 Economic Recovery In Southeast Asia. Retrieved from https://www.adb.org/sites/default/files/publication/639141/green-finance-post-covid-19-southeast-asia.pdf

87. BOI. 2019. Thailand Investment Review: Transport & Logistics, Vol. 29, December 2019. Retrieved from http://www.boi.go.th/upload/content/TIR6_2019_5e2e956d55219.pdf

88. PWC. 2021. Thailand's Infrastructure Market Update and Outlook. Retrieved from https://www.pwc.com/th/en/deals/capital-projects-n-infrastructure/thailand-infrastructure-market-update-and-outlook.html

89. ONEP, MNRE. 2015. Thailand's Intended Nationally Determined Contribution (INDC). Retrieved from https://www4.unfccc.int/sites/ndcstaging/PublishedDocuments/Thailand%20First/Thailand_INDC.pdf

90. World Wildlife Fund (WWF). 2020. Thailand NDC. Retrieved from https://wwf.panda.org/discover/our_focus/climate_and_energy_practice/ndcs_we_want/reviewed_ndcs_/thailand/

91. ONEP, MNRE. 2015. Thailand's Intended Nationally Determined Contribution (INDC). Retrieved from https://www4.unfccc.int/sites/ndcstaging/PublishedDocuments/Thailand%20First/Thailand_INDC.pdf

92. Ministry of Natural Resources and Environment (MNRE). 2021, National Action Plan on Plastic Waste Management in Thailand. Retrieved from https://www.iges.or.jp/sites/default/files/inline-files/S1-5_PPT_Thailand%20Plastic%20Action%20Plan.pdf

93. ONEP, MNRE. 2015. Thailand's Intended Nationally Determined Contribution (INDC). Retrieved from https://www4.unfccc.int/sites/ndcstaging/PublishedDocuments/Thailand%20First/Thailand_INDC.pdf

94. Thailand Development Research Institute (TDRI). 2021. Air pollution continues to kill: does Thailand's National Energy Plan offer hope? Retrieved from https://tdri.or.th/en/2021/09/fixing-thailands-killer-air-pollution/

95. Thai PBS World. 2021. Thailand vows to reach net zero carbon emissions by 2065 at COP26. Retrieved from https://www.thaipbsworld.com/thailand-vows-to-reach-net-zero-carbon-emissions-by-2065-at-cop26/

96. World Bank and ADB. 2021. Climate Risk Country Profile: Thailand. Retrieved from https://reliefweb.int/sites/reliefweb.int/files/resources/climate-risk-country-profile-thailand.pdf

97. ONEP, MNRE. 2015. Thailand's Intended Nationally Determined Contribution (INDC). Retrieved from https://www4.unfccc.int/sites/ndcstaging/PublishedDocuments/Thailand%20First/Thailand_INDC.pdf

98. https://d2rpq8wtqka5kg.cloudfront.net/389138/open20170919030300.pdf?Expires=1625996472&Signature=kJrAyDJrLDPtY1TfWD6ex~Fbkl-yqr4j8OMm0awJdNpcd3wqJn-jc8UeVL1COfZ-4RrsrllFyRhVXrjBUuWUK5CDezlw-A82s2f3-7WIQplWmtwYzDIEPMFYLzrfVVbGVN3Q3mtRFPmXvZsHU1wnoURFQKpcKlq0tbjiuuronJV1se-1~s7AjE3V2d3wZpt211EozrWo6OSByYtz6tOAIT4h56Ak4~nkS30BNCDH6jZp5DdkeQXAhV3RDeLq76gDn8QCue-vX8Twh3Z6CXAIpdzssCkD-1ZQ~YYdy5wa7kdHHkfdpse99Yk2K9cC~cKkPfpMXWkSSE7LBHRnbjuW4A__&Key-Pair-Id=APKAJVGCNMR6FQV6VYIA.

99. CBI. 2020. Sustainable Debt: Global State of the Market Report 2020. Retrieved from https://www.climatebonds.net/files/reports/cbi_sd_sotm_2020_04d.pdf

100. CBI. 2020. ASEAN Sustainable Finance State of the Market Report 2020. Retrieved from https://www.climatebonds.net/files/reports/asean-sotm-2020.pdf

101. The Thai Bond Market Association (ThaiBMA).2020. Foreign Investor. Retrieved from https://www.thaibma.or.th/EN/Foreign/ForeignPortal.aspx

102. BOT. Database on Rates of Exchange of Commercial Banks in Bangkok Metropolis (2002-present). Retrieved from https://www.bot.or.th/App/BTWS_STAT/statistics/ReportPage.aspx?reportID=123&language=eng

103. Thai Bond Market Association (ThaiBMA). 2020. Thai Bond Market Review. Retrieved from https://www.thaibma.or.th/Doc/annual/SummaryMarket2020.pdf

104. CBI. 2020. ASEAN Sustainable Finance State of the Market Report 2020. Retrieved from https://www.climatebonds.net/files/reports/asean-sotm-2020.pdf

105. The Securities and Exchange Commission (SEC). 2020. Guidelines on Issuance and Offer for Sale of Green Bond and Sustainability Bond. Retrieved from https://capital.sec.or.th/webapp//nrs/data/7874ae11.pdf. The guideline in original Thai language can be accessed at the following link: https://capital.sec.or.th/webapp/nrs/data/7874a11.pdf

106. Bangkok Post. 2021. ESG bond issuance likely to reach B100bn in 2021. Retrieved from https://www.bangkokpost.com/business/2122391/esg-bond-issuance-likely-to-reach-b100bn-this-year

107. OECD. 2021. Investment Policy Reviews: Thailand. Retrieved from https://www.oecd-ilibrary.org/sites/6091762f-en/index.html?itemId=/content/component/6091762f-en

108. ADB. 2018. ADB Invests 5 billion Thai Baht in B. Grimm Power's Green Bond to Develop Clean Energy in Thailand. Retrieved from https://www.adb.org/news/adb-invests-5-billion-thai-baht-bgrimm-power-s-green-bond-develop-clean-energy-thailand

109. International Finance Corporation (IFC). 2018. TMB Issues Thailand's First Green Bond for $60 Million. Retrieved from https://pressroom.ifc.org/all/pages/PressDetail.aspx?ID=18347

110. ADB. 2019. ADB Invests 3 Billion Thai Baht in Energy Absolute's Green Bond for Wind Farm Development. Retrieved from https://www.adb.org/news/adb-invests-3-billion-thai-baht-energy-absolutes-green-bond-wind-farm-development

111. Global Power Synergy Public Company Limited (GPSC). 2020. GPSC is Pleased with Investors' Confidence Resulting in the 6-Time Oversubscription or Over 30-Billion-Baht, Ready to Grow its Renewable Energy Business Under PTT Group's Power Business Expansion Plan. Retrieved from https://www.gpscgroup.com/en/investor-relations/newsroom/press-releases/790518/gpsc-is-pleased-with-investors-confidence-resulting-in-the-6-time-oversubscription-or-over-30-billion-baht-ready-to-grow-its-renewable-energy-business-under-ptt-groups-power-business-expansion-plan

112. PTT Public Company Limited (PTT). 2020. PTT Green Bond, DNV GL Pre Issuance Verification Assurance Opinion. Retrieved from https://pttdebenture.azurewebsites.net/src/upload/fckfiles/green-bond/20200908-ptt-debenture-second-party-opinion-report-pre-assurance-02.pdf

113. GPSC. 2020. GPSC is Pleased with Investors' Confidence Resulting in the 6-Time Oversubscription or Over 30-Billion-Baht, Ready to Grow its Renewable Energy Business Under PTT Group's Power Business Expansion Plan. Retrieved from https://www.gpscgroup.com/en/investor-relations/newsroom/press-releases/790518/gpsc-is-pleased-with-investors-confidence-resulting-in-the-6-time-oversubscription-or-over-30-billion-baht-ready-to-grow-its-renewable-energy-business-under-ptt-groups-power-business-expansion-plan

114. The Nation. 2020, BTSG issues Bt8.6bn in green bonds. Retrieved from https://www.nationthailand.com/news/30397264

115. Ministry of Finance (MOF), Thailand. 2020. Bank for Agriculture and Agricultural Cooperatives (BAAC)'s Inaugural Green Bond Issuance. Retrieved from https://media.thaigov.go.th/uploads/document/142/2020/08/pdf/Doc_20200820082924000000.pdf

116. CBI. 2020. Certification PTT Public Company. Retrieved from https://www.climatebonds.net/Certification/PTT%20Public%20Company

117. Ibid.

118. ADB, 2020. ADB and Green Finance Committee of China Society for Finance and Banking Co-host Webinar on Nature-Positive Stimulus Packages in COVID-19 Recovery. Retrieved from https://www.adb.org/news/adb-and-green-finance-committeechina-society-finance-and-banking-cohost-webinar-nature

119. International Capital Market Association (ICMA), 2020, Sustainability Bond Guidelines. Retrieved from https://www.icmagroup.org/sustainable-finance/the-principles-guidelines-and-handbooks/sustainability-bond-guidelines-sbg/

120. ASEAN Capital Markets Forum (ACMF), 2018. ASEAN Sustainability Bond Standards. Retrieved from https://www.theacmf.org/initiatives/sustainable-finance/asean-sustainability-bond-standards

121. ICMA. 2020. Social Bond Principles. Retrieved from https://www.icmagroup.org/assets/documents/Regulatory/Green-Bonds/June-2020/Social-Bond-PrinciplesJune-2020-090620.pdf

122. ACMF. 2018. ASEAN Social Bond Standards. Retrieved from https://www.sc.com.my/api/documentms/download.ashx?id=27ab0a48-b429-4874-93ae-35248ebea3e6

123. CBI. 2020. Thai Government Marks 2020 with Certified Sovereign Green Issuance: Commitment to Recovery, Sustainability, Infrastructure. Retrieved from https://www.climatebonds.net/2020/12/thai-govt-marks-2020-certified-sovereign-green-issuance-commitment-recovery-sustainability

124. Ibid.

125. ADB. 2020. ADB Supports Thailand's Green, Social, and Sustainability Bonds for COVID-19 Recovery. Retrieved from https://www.adb.org/news/adb-supports-thailand-green-social-and-sustainability-bonds-covid-19-recovery

126. Ibid.

127. National Housing Authority (NHA). Thailand. 2021. Sustainable Finance Framework, Sustainability bond 2021. Retrieved from https://www.nha.co.th/download/sustainable-finance-framework-nha-_eng-sustainability-bond-2021/

128. ADB. 2020. ADB Supports Thailand's Green, Social, and Sustainability Bonds for COVID-19 Recovery. Retrieved from https://www.adb.org/news/adb-supports-thailand-green-social-and-sustainability-bonds-covid-19-recovery

129. ADB. 2015. Fossil Fuel Subsidies in Thailand: Trends, Impacts, and Reform. Retrieved from https://www.adb.org/sites/default/files/publication/175455/fossil-fuel-subsidies-thailand.pdf

130. International Renewable Energy Agency (IRENA), 2017, Renewable Energy Outlook: Thailand. Retrieved from https://www.irena.org/-/media/files/irena/agency/publication/2017/nov/irena_outlook_thailand_2017.pdf

131. Ibid.

132. Ibid.

133. CBI. 2020. Financing Credible Transitions. Retrieved from https://www.climatebonds.net/files/reports/cbi_fincredtransitions_final.pdf

134. SEC. 2020. Sustainability development roadmap. Retrieved from https://www.sec.or.th/cgthailand/EN/pages/overview/sustainabledevelopmentroadmap.aspx

135. Task Force on Climate-Related Financial Disclosures (TCFD). Climate Change Presents Financial Risk to the Global Economy. Retrieved from https://www.fsb-tcfd.org

136. SEC. 2021. SEC becomes a supporter of the Task Force on Climate-Related Financial Disclosures. Retrieved from https://www.sec.or.th/EN/Pages/News_Detail.aspx?SECID=8746&NewsNo=11&NewsYear=2021&Lang=EN

137. FPO, BOT, SEC, OIC, and SET. 2021. Sustainable Finance Initiatives for Thailand. Retrieved from https://www.bot.or.th/Thai/SustainableBanking/Documents/Sustainable_Finance_Initiatives_for_Thailand.pdf

138. SET. 2019. ESG & Responsible Investing in Thailand, a presentation by Manpong Senanarong (Senior Executive Vice President, SET) at the ASEAN Institutional Investors Forum 2019. Retrieved from https://www.setsustainability.com/download/jsfgbpi6nzawm8l

139. CFA Institute. 2019. ESG Disclosures in Asia Pacific: A Review of ESG Disclosure Regimes for Listed Companies in Selected Markets. Retrieved from https://www.arx.cfa/-/media/regional/arx/post-pdf/2019/08/04/esg-disclosures-in-asia-pacific.ashx

140. ASEAN CSR Network and NUS Business School, National University of Singapore. 2018. Sustainability Reporting in ASEAN Countries. Retrieved from https://www.asean-csr-network.org/c/images/Resources/Reports/2018_Sustainability_Reporting_in_ASEAN_Countries.pdf

141. SET. 2021. SETTHSI Index. Retrieved from https://www.set.or.th/dat/report/product/SETTHSI_MonthlyReport_20210730.pdf

142. ACGA and CLSA. 2018. CG Watch, 2018: Hard Decisions: Asia Faces Tough Choices in CG Reform. Retrieved from https://www.acga-asia.org/cgwatch-detail.php?id=362

143. CFA Institute. 2019. ESG Disclosures in Asia Pacific: A Review of ESG Disclosure Regimes for Listed Companies in Selected Markets. Retrieved from https://www.arx.cfa/-/media/regional/arx/post-pdf/2019/08/04/esg-disclosures-in-asia-pacific.ashx

144. Sustainable Stock Exchange Initiative (SSE). 2019. How Stock Exchanges Can Grow Green Finance. Retrieved from https://sseinitiative.org/wp-content/uploads/2019/12/SSE-Green-Finance-Guidance-.pdf

145. SET. 2020. Thai listed companies mark ASEAN's top inclusions in Dow Jones Sustainability World Index (DJSI World). Retrieved from https://www.set.or.th/set/pdfnews.do?newsId=16054795884190&sequence=0

146. SET. Sustainability Disclosure & Reporting. Retrieved from https://www.setsustainability.com/page/disclosure

147. National Corporate Governance Committee. 2017. Thai Corporate Governance Code for Listed Companies 2017. Retrieved from https://ecgi.global/node/6197

148. BOT. Bank of Thailand's Strategic Plan (2020–2022): Central Bank in a Transformative World. Retrieved from https://www.bot.or.th/English/AboutBOT/RolesAndHistory/DocLib_StrategicPlan/BOT-StrategicPlan2020to2022-eng.pdf

149. FPO, BOT, SEC, OIC, and SET. 2021. Sustainable Finance Initiatives for Thailand. Retrieved from https://www.bot.or.th/Thai/SustainableBanking/Documents/Sustainable_Finance_Initiatives_for_Thailand.pdf

150. The Thai bankers Association (TBA), 2019, Sustainable Banking Guidelines Responsible Lending. Retrieved from https://www.tba.or.th/wp-content/uploads/2019/08/Guidelines-ResponsibleLending.pdf

151. CBI. 2020, Green, Social, and Sustainability (GSS) Bonds Database.

152. Ministry of Energy (MOE), Thailand. 2014. Energy Efficiency Promotion Measures in Thailand, a presentation by Prasert Sinsukprasert, MOE, at the 5th International Energy Forum For Sustainable Development 4-7 November 2014 Tunisia. Retrieved from https://unece.org/fileadmin/DAM/energy/se/pp/eneff/5th_Forum_Tunisia_Nov.14/4_November/Prasert_Sinsukprasert.pdf

153. Siam Commercial Bank (SCB). 2020. SME Go Green Loan from SCB lets SMEs go lean and green, while boosting sustainability and a positive economy. Retrieved from https://www.scb.co.th/en/about-us/news/jul-2020/nws-sme-go-green.html

154. ASEAN Centre for Energy. 2019. Energy Efficiency Financing Guideline in Thailand. Retrieved from https://aeep.aseanenergy.org/wp-content/uploads/2019/05/EEF-Guideline-in-Thailand.pdf

155. Royal Thai Embassy, Washington D.C., 2020. Energy Ministry ready to fund 1,000 renewables projects. Retrieved from https://thaiembdc.org/2020/09/11/energy-ministry-ready-to-fund-1000-renewables-projects/

156. ADB. 2019. ASEAN Infrastructure Fund: Financing Infrastructure for Growth and Development. Retrieved from https://www.adb.org/publications/asean-infrastructure-fund-brochure

157. ADB. ASEAN Infrastructure Fund Projects. Retrieved from https://www.adb.org/projects/fund/ASEAN%20Infrastructure%20Fund

158. OECD. Blended Finance Principles. Retrieved from https://www.oecd.org/dac/financing-sustainable-development/blended-finance-principles/

159. ADB. 2019. New Facility to Mobilize $1 Billion for ASEAN Green Infrastructure. Retrieved from https://www.adb.org/news/new-facility-mobilize-1-billion-asean-green-infrastructure

160. Ibid.
161. 68 IFC. 2019. IFC and Bank of Thailand Join Hands to Accelerate Sustainable Finance in Thailand. Retrieved from https://pressroom.ifc.org/all/pages/PressDetail.aspx?ID=17697
162. ADB. 2021. Thailand: Country Partnership Strategy (2021–2025). Retrieved from https://www.adb.org/documents/thailand-country-partnership-strategy-2021-2025
163. ADB. 2021, ADB Green Bond: Newsletter and Impact Report. Retrieved from https://www.adb.org/sites/default/files/publication/297141/adb-green-bond-newsletter-2021.pdf
164. ADB. 2021. Thailand, 2021–2025—Prosperity and Sustainability through Knowledge and Private-Sector-Led Growth. Retrieved from https://www.adb.org/sites/default/files/institutional-document/703071/tha-cps-2021-2025.pdf
165. https://www.fsb-tcfd.org
166. https://www.sec.or.th/TH/Documents/KnowledgeBase/SustainableFinanceInitiativesforThailand.pdf
167. http://ccap.org/assets/CCAP-Booklet_Thailand.pdf
168. ASEAN Centre for Energy (2019). Energy Efficiency Financing Guideline in Thailand. https://agep.aseanenergy.org/wp-content/uploads/2019/05/EEF-Guideline-in-Thailand.pdf
169. ADB. 2020. ACGF Overview. https://www.adb.org/what-wedo/funds/asean-catalytic-green-finance-facility/overview
170. Climate Bonds, ADB, and the Sustainable Finance Institute ASEAN (SFIA). 2020. Green Finance Capital Market Approaches to Support Post COVID Economic Recovery.
171. https://www.adb.org/news/partners-pledge-665-million-support-green-recovery-asean
172. CBI.2021. Climate Bonds Taxonomy. Retrieved from https://www.climatebonds.net/standard/taxonomy
173. CBI. 2021. Climate Bonds Standard and Certification Scheme. Retrieved from https://www.climatebonds.net/standard
174. The Energy Policy and Planning Office (EPPO), MOE. 2021. Energy Statistics. Retrieved from http://www.eppo.go.th/index.php/en/en-energystatistics/summary-statistic?orders%5BpublishUp%5D=publishUp&issearch=1
175. IEA. Key Energy Statistics, Electricity Generation by Source of Energy, 1990–2019. Retrieved from https://www.iea.org/countries/thailand
176. U.S. Energy Information Administration (EIA). Analysis: Thailand. Retrieved from https://www.eia.gov/international/analysis/country/THA
177. IEA. Thailand's Energy Polies. Retrieved from https://www.iea.org/countries/thailand
178. EPPO, MOE. 2019. Thailand's Energy 4.0, a presentation by Dr. Twarath Sutabutr, MOE. Retrieved from https://iecc.energy.go.th/wp-content/uploads/2019/03/00_Energy-4.pdf
179. Pranadi, Aloysius Damar (ASEAN Center for Energy). 2016, The Current Status of RE and its Target in ASEAN Member States. Retrieved from https://aseanenergy.org/the-current-status-of-re-and-its-target-in-asean-member-states/
180. IRENA. 2021. Renewable Energy Statistics 2021. Retrieved from https://www.irena.org/publications/2021/Aug/Renewable-energy-statistics-2021
181. 89 Climate Scorecard. 2019. Thailand: The Government Is Taking Steps To Increase Renewable Energy, But Must Do More To Engage Key Stakeholders In The Process. Retrieved from https://www.climatescorecard.org/2019/11/the-government-is-taking-steps-to-increase-renewable-energy-but-must-do-more-to-engage-key-stakeholders-in-the-process/
182. IRENA. 2017. Thailand Renewable Energy Outlook. Retrieved from https://www.irena.org/_/media/Files/IRENA/Agency/Publication/2017/Nov/IRENA_Outlook_Thailand_2017.pdf
183. Ibid.
184. ADB. Thailand: Southern Thailand Wind Power and Battery Energy Storage Project. Retrieved from https://www.adb.org/projects/53174-001/main#project-pds
185. Energy Storage News. 2020. Asian Development Bank signs US$7.2m loan for Thailand wind-plus-battery project. Retrieved from https://www.energy-storage.news/asian-development-bank-signs-us7-2m-loan-for-thailand-wind-plus-battery-project/
186. Global Wind Energy Council (GEWC). 2019. Wind industry calls for additional 7 GW of wind energy to be installed in Thailand by 2037. Retrieved from https://gwec.net/wind-industry-calls-for-additional-7-gw-of-wind-energy-to-be-installed-in-thailand-by-2037/
187. Krungsri Bank. 2021. Industry Outlook 2021-2023: Power Generation. Retrieved from https://www.krungsri.com/en/research/industry/industry-outlook/Energy-Utilities/Power-Generation/IO/io-power-generation-21
188. IRENA. 2017. Thailand Renewable Energy Outlook. Retrieved from https://www.irena.org/_/media/Files/IRENA/Agency/Publication/2017/Nov/IRENA_Outlook_Thailand_2017.pdf
189. Krungsri Bank. 2021. Industry Outlook 2021-2023: Power Generation. Retrieved from https://www.krungsri.com/en/research/industry/industry-outlook/Energy-Utilities/Power-Generation/IO/io-power-generation-21
190. BlombergNEF, 2019. The Clean Technology Fund and Concessional Finance: Lessons Learned and Strategies Moving Forward Retrieved from https://data.bloomberglp.com/professional/sites/24/BNEF_The-Clean-Technology-Fund-and-Concessional-Finance-2019-Report.pdf
191. OECD. 2021. Investment Policy Reviews: Thailand. Retrieved from https://www.oecd-ilibrary.org/sites/6091762f-en/index.html?itemId=/content/component/6091762f-en
192. Frankfurt School -UNEP Collaborating Centre for Climate & Sustainable Energy Finance .2012. National Climate Finance Institutions Support Programme, Case Study: The Thai Energy Efficiency Revolving Fund. Retrieved from https://unfccc.int/files/cooperation_and_support/financial_mechanism/standing_committee/application/pdf/fs-unep_thai_eerf_final_2012.pdf
193. Royal Thai Embassy, Washington D.C., 2020. Energy Ministry ready to fund 1,000 renewables projects. Retrieved from https://thaiembdc.org/2020/09/11/energy-ministry-ready-to-fund-1000-renewables-projects/
194. Climate Investment Funds (CIF) Investing in Thailand. Retrieved from https://www.climateinvestmentfunds.org/country/thailand
195. CBI. 2020. ASEAN Sustainable Finance State of the Market Report 2020. Retrieved from https://www.climatebonds.net/files/reports/asean-sotm-2020.pdf
196. ADB. 2018. ADB Invests 5 billion Thai Baht in B. Grimm Power's Green Bond to Develop Clean Energy in Thailand. Retrieved from https://www.adb.org/news/adb-invests-5-billion-thai-baht-bgrimm-power-s-green-bond-develop-clean-energy-thailand
197. ADB. 2021. ADB Green Bond Newsletter and Impact Report 2021. Retrieved from https://www.adb.org/publications/adb-green-bonds
198. IRENA. Solar Energy. Retrieved from https://www.irena.org/solar
199. IRENA. Wind Energy. Retrieved from https://www.irena.org/wind
200. IRENA. 2021, World Adds Record New Renewable Energy Capacity in 2020. Retrieved from https://www.irena.org/newsroom/pressreleases/2021/Apr/World-Adds-Record-New-Renewable-Energy-Capacity-in-2020
201. IEA. 2020. Hydropower. Retrieved from https://www.iea.org/fuels-and-technologies/hydropower
202. United Nations Framework Convention on Climate Change (UNFCCC). 2016. Railway Sector on Track to Achieve Low Carbon Goals. Retrieved from https://unfccc.int/news/railway-sector-on-track-to-acheive-low-carbon-goals
203. UNFCCC. 2015. World Needs to Manage Water More Sustainably. Retrieved from https://unfccc.int/news/world-needs-to-manage-water-more-sustainably
204. GreenBiz. 2016. How the Paris Agreement sparked green-building progress. Retrieved from https://www.greenbiz.com/article/how-paris-agreement-sparked-green-building-progress
205. Project Drawdown (n/a). Electricity Generation Geothermal. Retrieved from https://www.drawdown.org/solutions/electricity-generation/geothermal
206. International Energy Agency (2019). Hydropower. Retrieved from https://www.iea.org/fuels-and-technologies/hydropower
207. UNFCCC (2018). Clean Energy Transition Needs to Accelerate. Retrieved from https://unfccc.int/news/clean-energy-transition-needs-to-accelerate
208. UNFCCC (2016). Railway Sector on Track to Acheive Low Carbon Goals. Retrieved from https://unfccc.int/news/railway-sector-on-track-to-acheive-low-carbon-goals
209. UNFCCC (2015). World Needs to Manage Water more sustainably. Retrieved from https://unfccc.int/news/world-needs-to-manage-water-more-sustainably
210. Greenbiz (2016). How the Paris Agreement sparked green-building progress. Retrieved from https://www.greenbiz.com/article/how-paris-agreement-sparked-green-building-progress
211. IEA. Key Energy Indicators. Retrieved from https://www.iea.org/countries/thailand
212. ADB. Thailand Green Bond Project (RRP THA 52292). Retrieved from https://www.adb.org/sites/default/files/linked-documents/52292-001-sd-03.pdf
213. B.Grimm Power. 2021. B.Grimm Power: Q1'2021 Opportunity Day. Retrieved from https://bgrim.listedcompany.com/misc/presentation/20210617-bgrim-oppday-1q2021.pdf
214. ADB. 2020. Extended Annual Review Report: Chaiyaphum Wind Farm Company Limited Subyai Wind Power Project (Thailand). Retrieved from https://www.adb.org/sites/default/files/project-documents/48233/48233-001-xarr-en.pdf
215. ADB. 2019. Environmental and Social Compliance Audit, Energy Absolute Green Bond for Wind Power Project, Thailand. Retrieved from https://www.adb.org/sites/default/files/project-documents/53255/53255-001-escar-en.pdf
216. Energy Absolute Public Company Limited. 2018. "Energy Absolute Public Company Limited" (presentation on corporate information). Retrieved from https://www.energyabsolute.co.th/calendar/presentation/20180904095700.pdf
217. ADB. 2019. Report and Recommendation of the President to the Board of Directors: Proposed Debt Investment, Energy Absolute Public Company Limited Energy Absolute Green Bond for Wind Power Project (Thailand). Retrieved from https://www.adb.org/sites/default/files/project-documents/53255/53255-001-rrp-en.pdf
218. ADB. 2020. Report and Recommendation of the President to the Board of Directors: Proposed Loan Energy Absolute Public Company Limited Green Loan for Renewable Energy and Electric Vehicle Charging Network (Thailand). Retrieved from https://www.adb.org/sites/default/files/project-documents/54268/54268-001-rrp-en.pdf
219. Ministry of Transport (MOT), Thailand. 2013. Thailand's Environmental Sustainable Transport Master Plan. Retrieved from https://www.uncrd.or.jp/content/documents/7EST-B1G4-6.pdf
220. GIZ. Thailand Clean Mobility Programme (Thailand Component of Global Project Transfer III). Retrieved from https://www.giz.de/en/worldwide/83111.html
221. United Nations Environmental Programme (UNEP). 2019. Air pollution is choking Bangkok, but a solution is in reach. Retrieved from https://www.unep.org/news-and-stories/story/air-pollution-choking-bangkok-solution-reach
222. Office of Transport and Traffic Policy and Planning (OTP), MOT.2019. Intelligent Transport System (ITS) in Thailand. Retrieved from https://www.unescap.org/sites/default/files/Country%20presentation%20-%20Thailand_3.pdf
223. OTP, MOT. 2017. Railway development and long term plan in Thailand, a presentation by Mr. Chaiwat Thongkamkoon (Director General, OTP). Retrieved from https://www.otp.go.th/uploads/tiny_uploads/PDF/2560-11/25601124-RaiwalDevOTP.pdf
224. BOI. 2019. Thailand Investment Review: Transport & Logistics, Vol. 29, December 2019. Retrieved from http://www.boi.go.th/upload/content/TIR6_2019_5e2e956d55219.pdf
225. BOI. Additional Investment Policies and Promotional Measures.Retrieved from https://www.boi.go.th/index.php?page=add_investment
226. Sitthiyot, Thitithep. 2017. The Truth about Thailand's Transport Infrastructure Development and Financing. Nomura Journal Of Asian Capital Markets. Spring 2017 Vol.1/No.2, pp.38-43. Retrieved from https://www.nomurafoundation.or.jp/wordpress/wp-content/uploads/2017/04/NJACM1-1SP17-08.pdf
227. SEPO. 2018. The Launch of Thailand Future Fund, a presentation by Prapas Kong-led, Director-General of SEPO, given at "Thailand Focus 2018: The Future is Now" 29th August 2018, Grand Hyatt Erawan Bangkok Hotel. Retrieved from http://www.sepo.go.th/assets/document/file/Thailand%20Focus%202018%20v20-8-2018%20editted.pdf
228. Bank of Thailand (BOT). Database on Government Domestic Debt Outstanding Classified by Holders. Retrieved from https://www.bot.or.th/App/BTWS_STAT/statistics/ReportPage.aspx?reportID=40&language=eng
229. PPP Knowledge Lab. Thailand. Retrieved from https://pppknowledgelab.org/countries/thailand
230. Sitthiyot, Thitithep. 2017. The Truth about Thailand's Transport Infrastructure Development and Financing. Nomura Journal Of Asian Capital Markets. Spring 2017 Vol.1/No.2, pp.38-43. Retrieved from https://www.nomurafoundation.or.jp/wordpress/wp-content/uploads/2017/04/NJACM1-1SP17-08.pdf
231. SEPO. 2018. The Launch of Thailand Future Fund, a presentation by Prapas Kong-led, Director-General of SEPO, given at "Thailand Focus 2018: The Future is Now" 29th August 2018, Grand Hyatt Erawan Bangkok Hotel. Retrieved from http://www.sepo.go.th/assets/document/file/Thailand%20Focus%202018%20v20-8-2018%20editted.pdf
232. Ibid.
233. BTS Group Holdings Public Company Limited. 2021. Green Bond Report (August 2021). Retrieved from https://www.btsgroup.co.th/storage/download/sustainability/green-bond/bts-green-bond-report-2021-en.pdf
234. BTS Group Holdings Public Company Limited. 2020. Letter on "Issuance and offering of green bond of the Company" (Ref. No. BTS 15849/2020). Retrieved from https://www.set.or.th/dat/news/202011/20120414.pdf
235. PDMO, MOF. 2021 "2020 Sustainability Bond Interim Report A Year of Accomplishments". Retrieved from https://www.pdmo.go.th/pdmomedia/documents/2021/Feb/Minister%20Approved%202020.pdf
236. Ibid.
237. Ibid.
238. Mass Rapid Transit Authority of Thailand (MRTA). MRT Civil Work Progress ,October 2021. Retrieved from https://www.mrta.co.th/en/projectelectrictrain/construction_progress_report/
239. Railway Technology. MRTA Pink Line, Bangkok. Retrieved from https://www.railway-technology.com/projects/mrta-pink-line-bangkok/
240. MRTA. 2017. "Contracts Signed for Bangkok's Pink and Yellow Monorail Lines". Retrieved from https://mrta-yellowline.com/wp/en/contracts-signed-for-bangkoks-pink-and-yellow-monorail-lines/
241. MRTA. The Pink Line. Retrieved from https://www.mrta.co.th/en/projectelectrictrain/bangkok-and-vicinities/pinkline/
242. PPP Knowledge Lab. Thailand. Retrieved from https://pppknowledgelab.org/countries/thailand
243. MRTA. The Yellow Line. Retrieved from https://www.mrta.co.th/en/projectelectrictrain/bangkok-and-vicinities/yellowline/
244. ADB. Thailand: Bangkok Mass Rapid Transit Project (Pink and Yellow Lines) Retrieved from https://www.adb.org/projects/51274-001/main#project-pds
245. Bangkok Post. 2017. Bank trio ally for monorail financing. Retrieved from https://www.bangkokpost.com/business/1340303/bank-trio-ally-for-monorail-financing
246. BTS Group Holdings Public Company Limited. 2020. Green Bond Report. Retrieved from https://www.btsgroup.co.th/storage/download/sustainability/green-bond/bts-green-bond-report-2020-en.pdf
247. BTS Group Holdings Public Company Limited. 2020. Letter on "Issuance and offering of green bond of the Company" (Ref. No. BTS 15849/2020). Retrieved from https://www.set.or.th/dat/news/202011/20120414.pdf
248. ADB. Thailand: Bangkok Mass Rapid Transit Project (Pink and Yellow Lines)(Project Overview). Retrieved from https://www.adb.org/projects/51274-001/main#project-overview

249. MRTA. The MRT Orange Line (East) Project-Thailand Cultural Center-Min Buri (Suwinthawong): Construction Progress. Retrieved from https://www.mrta-orangelineeast.com/en/home_progress
250. MRTA. The MRT Orange Line (East) Project-Thailand Cultural Center-Min Buri (Suwinthawong): Project Details. Retrieved from https://www.mrta-orangelineeast.com/en/route
251. MRTA. The Orange Line. Retrieved from https://www.mrta.co.th/en/projectelectrictrain/bangkok-and-vicinities/orangeline/
252. MRTA. The MRT Orange Line (East) Project-Thailand Cultural Center-Min Buri (Suwinthawong): Project Details (Project Investments) Retrieved from https://mrta-orangelineeast.com/en/invest
253. PDMO, MOF. 2021 "2020 Sustainability Bond Interim Report A Year of Accomplishments". Retrieved from https://www.pdmo.go.th/pdmomedia/documents/2021/Feb/Minister%20Approved%202020.pdf
254. Eastern Economic Corridor (EEC) Office. Retrieved from https://www.eeco.or.th/en/news/351
255. PWC. 2021. Thailand's Infrastructure Market Update and Outlook. Retrieved from https://www.pwc.com/th/en/deals/capital-projects-n-infrastructure/thailand-infrastructure-market-update-and-outlook.html
256. BOT. Database on Rates of Exchange of Commercial Banks in Bangkok Metropolis (2002-present). Retrieved from https://www.bot.or.th/App/BTWS_STAT/statistics/ReportPage.aspx?reportID=123&language=eng
257. SEPO. 2020. Public-Private Partnership Project Delivery Plan 2020 – 2027. Retrieved from http://www.ppp.sepo.go.th/tinymce/plugins/filemanager/thumbs/PPP%20Delivery%20Plan%202020-2027_Mar2020%20(EN).pdf
258. SEPO. 2021. Public-Private Partnership Project Delivery Plan 2020 – 2027 (Updated as of August 2021) (In Thai). Retrieved from http://www.ppp.sepo.go.th/tinymce/plugins/filemanager/thumbs/แผนการจัดทำโครงการร่วมลงทุน%202564-2%20(ลงเว็บไซต์).pdf
259. ADB 2017. Thailand: Bangkok Mass Rapid Transit South Purple Line Project (Technical Assistance Report). Retrieved from https://www.adb.org/sites/default/files/project-documents/51048/51048-001-tar-en.pdf
260. MRTA. The MRT Purple Line Project: Tao Pun - Rat Burana (Kanchanaphisek Road) Section. Retrieved from https://www.mrta.co.th/en/projectelectrictrain/bangkok-and-vicinities/purpleline/#head4
261. MDPI. Special Issue Advances and Challenges in the Sustainable Water Management. Retrieved from https://www.mdpi.com/journal/sustainability/special_issues/sustainable_water
262. OpenDevelopment Thailand. 2018. SDG6 Clean Water and Sanitation. Retrieved from https://thailand.opendevelopmentmekong.net/topics/sdg-6-clean-water-and-sanitation/
263. Office of the National Water Resources (ONWR), Prime Minister's Office. The National Water Resources Management Strategies. Retrieved from http://www.onwr.go.th/en/?page_id=4207
264. Mahanakorn Partners Group (MPG). 2020. Thailand Expands Activities Subject to the Thai PPP Act. Retrieved from https://mahanakornpartners.com/thailand-expands-activities-subject-to-the-thai-ppp-act/
265. SEPO. 2020. Public-Private Partnership Project Delivery Plan 2020 – 2027. Retrieved from http://www.ppp.sepo.go.th/tinymce/plugins/filemanager/thumbs/PPP%20Delivery%20Plan%202020-2027_Mar2020%20(EN).pdf
266. EEC Office. 2020. U-Tapao International Airport and Eastern Airport City - EEC Water Management Plan - Renewable Energy (Solar Energy) Project. Retrieved from https://eeco.or.th/en/news/NO-1-2020-The-Eastern-Economic-Corridor-Policy-Committee-1st-issue
267. World Today News. 2021. Big Pok, the silent ambush of the 65th year, a giant project bound over 21,814 million years. Retrieved from https://www.world-today-news.com/big-pok-the-silent-ambush-of-the-65th-year-a-giant-project-bound-over-21814-million-years/
268. OECD. 2019. Making Blended Finance Work for Water and Sanitation: Unlocking Finance for SDG 6. Retrieved from https://www.oecd.org/environment/resources/Making-Blended-Finance-Work-for-Water-and-Sanitation-Policy-Highlights.pdf
269. High-Level Panel on Water (HLPW). Water Investment and Infrastructure: Recommendations. Retrieved from https://sustainabledevelopment.un.org/content/documents/hlpwater/08-WaterInfrastInvest.pdf
270. World Bank. Thai Tap Water (TTW) Water Production and Distribution Concession. Retrieved from https://ppi.worldbank.org/en/snapshots/project/thai-tap-water-ttw-water-production-and-distribution-concession-4949
271. BOT. Database on Rates of Exchange of Commercial Banks in Bangkok Metropolis (2002-present). Retrieved from https://www.bot.or.th/App/BTWS_STAT/statistics/ReportPage.aspx?reportID=123&language=eng
272. The Government Public Relations Department, Office of the Prime Minister. 2019. Royally Initiated Lam Nam Chi Reservoir Project Wins Cabinet Approval. Retrieved from https://thailand.prd.go.th/ewt_news.php?nid=7521&filename=index
273. BOT. Database on Rates of Exchange of Commercial Banks in Bangkok Metropolis (2002-present). Retrieved from https://www.bot.or.th/App/BTWS_STAT/statistics/ReportPage.aspx?reportID=123&language=eng
274. SEPO. 2020. Public-Private Partnership Project Delivery Plan 2020 – 2027. Retrieved from http://www.ppp.sepo.go.th/tinymce/plugins/filemanager/thumbs/PPP%20Delivery%20Plan%202020-2027_Mar2020%20(EN).pdf
275. World Today News. 2021. Big Pok, the silent ambush of the 65th year, a giant project bound over 21,814 million years. Retrieved from https://www.world-today-news.com/big-pok-the-silent-ambush-of-the-65th-year-a-giant-project-bound-over-21814-million-years/
276. BOT. Database on Rates of Exchange of Commercial Banks in Bangkok Metropolis (2002-present). Retrieved from https://www.bot.or.th/App/BTWS_STAT/statistics/ReportPage.aspx?reportID=123&language=eng
277. Bangkok Post. 2021. Anti-flooding plans agreed. Retrieved from https://www.bangkokpost.com/thailand/general/2051119/anti-flooding-plans-agreed
278. Thailand Environment Institute (TEI). 2020. Solid Waste During COVID-19. Retrieved from http://www.tei.or.th/en/blog_detail.php?blog_id=49
279. Office of Natural Resources and Environmental Policy and Planning (ONEP), Ministry of Natural Resources and Environmental (MNRE).2020. Thailand Third Biennial Update Report. Retrieved from https://unfccc.int/sites/default/files/resource/BUR3_Thailand_251220%20.pdf
280. TEI. 2020. "Solid Waste During COVID-19". Retrieved from http://www.tei.or.th/en/blog_detail.php?blog_id=49
281. IUCN-EA-QUANTIS. 2020. National Guidance for plastic pollution hotspotting and shaping action, Country report Thailand. Retrieved from https://www.iucn.org/sites/dev/files/content/documents/thailand_final-report_2020_compressed.pdf
282. ONEP. 2020. Thailand Third Biennial Update Report. Retrieved from https://unfccc.int/sites/default/files/resource/BUR3_Thailand_251220%20.pdf
283. The Government Public Relations Department, Office of the Prime Minister. 2021. Strategic Plan to Move Thailand Forward with BCG Economy Model. Retrieved from https://thailand.prd.go.th/1700/ewt/thailand/ewt_news.php?nid=10661&filename=index
284. Pollution Control Department, MNRE. 2019. 3R in Thailand: Policy Plans and Practices, a presentation by Pralong Dumrongthai (Director General, Pollution Control Department) at Plenary Session 1 on "Circular economy towards sufficiency economy- Implications for SDGs" at the Ninth Regional 3R Forum in Asia and the Pacific, 4-6 March 2019, Royal Orchid Sheraton Hotel & Towers, Bangkok, Thailand. Retrieved from https://www.uncrd.or.jp/content/documents/7554PS-1-PPT-3.pdf
285. The Government Public Relations Department, Office of the Prime Minister. 2029. Roadmap on Plastic Waste Management. Retrieved from https://thailand.prd.go.th/1700/ewt/thailand/ewt_news.php?nid=7831&filename=index
286. BOI. 2019. Thailand Investment Review: Circular Economy Shaping a Sustainable Future. Vol. 29. November 2019. Retrieved from https://www.boi.go.th/upload/content/TIR5_2019_5e2e95134a76b.pdf
287. Babel, S., Ta, A. T., & Habarakada Liyanage, T. U. 2020. Current Situation and Challenges of Waste Management in Thailand. In A. Pariatamby, F. Shahul Hamid, & M. Bhatti (Ed.), Sustainable Waste Management Challenges in Developing Countries (pp. 409-440). IGI Global. http://doi:10.4018/978-1-7998-0198-6.ch017. Retrieved from https://www.researchgate.net/publication/338308819_Current_Situation_and_Challenges_of_Waste_Management_in_Thailand
288. Global Power Synergy Public Company Limited (GPSC). 2018. Pracharat Helps Manage Waste Management In Sustainable Ways Rayong Province, Rayong Provincial Administration Have Joined Hand With GPSC to Create Comprehensive Waste Management Strategy with Refuse Derived Fuel (RDF) Technology. Retrieved from https://www.gpscgroup.com/en/investor-relations/newsroom/press-releases/668277/pracharat-helps-manage-waste-management-in-sustainable-ways-rayong-province-rayong-provincial-administration-have-joined-hand-with-gpsc-to-create-comprehensive-waste-management-strategy-with-refuse-derived-fuel-rdf-technology
289. International Finance Corporation (IFC). 2018. TMB Issues Thailand's First Green Bond for $60 Million. Retrieved from https://pressroom.ifc.org/all/pages/PressDetail.aspx?ID=18347
290. GPSC. 2020. GPSC is Pleased with Investors' Confidence Resulting in the 6-Time Oversubscription or Over 30-Billion-Baht, Ready to Grow its Renewable Energy Business Under PTT Group's Power Business Expansion Plan. Retrieved from https://www.gpscgroup.com/en/investor-relations/newsroom/press-releases/790518/gpsc-is-pleased-with-investors-confidence-resulting-in-the-6-time-oversubscription-or-over-30-billion-baht-ready-to-grow-its-renewable-energy-business-under-ptt-groups-power-business-expansion-plan
291. GPSC. 2016. Corporate Presentation Thailand Focus 2016. Retrieved from https://investor.gpscgroup.com/misc/presentation/20160901-gpsc-roadshow-thailand-focus-2016.pdf
292. BOT. Database on Rates of Exchange of Commercial Banks in Bangkok Metropolis (2002-present). Retrieved from https://www.bot.or.th/App/BTWS_STAT/statistics/ReportPage.aspx?reportID=123&language=eng
293. GPSC. 2016. Corporate Presentation Thailand Focus 2016. Retrieved from https://investor.gpscgroup.com/misc/presentation/20160901-gpsc-roadshow-thailand-focus-2016.pdf
294. GPSC. 2021. Green Debentures Report 2020. Retrieved from https://www.gpscgroup.com/storage/download/investor-relations/debenture-information/20210322-gpsc-green-debentures-report-en.pdf
295. The Nation. 2020. Rayong pushes for 10MW waste-to-energy plant ahead of EEC growth. Retrieved from https://www.nationthailand.com/noname/30392003
296. Hitachizosen. 2019. Order received to build and install equipment for energy-from-waste plant in Rayong Province, Thailand. Retrieved from https://www.hitachizosen.co.jp/english/newsroom/news/release/2019/20190703_001388.html
297. UNEP and Institute for Global Environmental Strategies (IGES). 2020. CCET guideline series on intermediate municipal solid waste treatment technologies: Waste-to-Energy Incineration. Retrieved from https://www.iges.or.jp/en/publication_documents/pub/policysubmission/en/10877/WtEI_guideline_web_200615.pdf
298. Suez Group. 2020. SUEZ opens its first recycling plant in Thailand dedicated to reversing plastic pollution crisis in Asia. Retrieved from https://www.suez.com/en/news/press-releases/suez-opens-its-first-plastic-recycling-plant-in-thailand
299. Suez Group. 2019. Chonburi Clean Energy (CCE) inaugurates its waste-to-energy power plant. Retrieved from https://www.suez-asia.com/en-cn/news/press-releases/chonburi-clean-energy-inaugurates-its-wte-power-plant
300. Global Alliance for Buildings and Construction (Global ABC), International Energy Agency (IEA) and the United Nations Environment Programme (UNEP) .2019. 2019 global status report for buildings and construction: Towards a zero-emission, efficient and resilient buildings and construction sector. Retrieved from https://www.worldgbc.org/sites/default/files/2019%20Global%20Status%20Report%20for%20Buildings%20and%20Construction.pdf
301. Worldometers. Thailand CO2 Emissions. Retrieved from https://www.worldometers.info/co2-emissions/thailand-co2-emissions/
302. Sugsaisakon, Sittisak, and Suthirat Kittipongvises. 2021. Citywide Energy-Related CO2 Emissions and Sustainability Assessment of the Development of Low-Carbon Policy in Chiang Mai, Thailand. Sustainability 13, no. 12: 6789. https://doi.org/10.3390/su13126789.
303. Lorenz & Partners. 2020. Green Building in Thailand. Retrieved from https://lorenz-partners.com/download/thailand/NL208E-Green-Building-in-Thailand-Feb20.pdf
304. GPSC. 2016. Corporate Presentation Thailand Focus 2016. Retrieved from https://investor.gpscgroup.com/misc/presentation/20160901-gpsc-roadshow-thailand-focus-2016.pdf
305. Lohmeng, A., Sudasna, K., & Tondee, T. (2017). State of The Art of Green Building Standards and Certification System Development in Thailand. Energy Procedia, 138, 417–422. https://doi.org/10.1016/j.egypro.2017.10.188
306. Electricity Generating Authority of Thailand (EGAT) 2020. EGAT and NHA develop Label No.5 House towards Smart and Sustainable Community. Retrieved from https://www.egat.co.th/en/news-announcement/news-release/egat-and-nha-develop-label-no-5-house-towards-smart-and-sustainable-community
307. The Business Times. 2021. Sustainable real estate asset investments to grow in South-east Asia. Retrieved from https://www.businesstimes.com.sg/real-estate/sustainable-real-estate-asset-investments-to-grow-in-south-east-asia
308. Green Building Information Gateway (GBIG). Thailand. Retrieved from http://www.gbig.org/places/886
309. Lohmeng, A., Sudasna, K., & Tondee, T. (2017). State of The Art of Green Building Standards and Certification System Development in Thailand. Energy Procedia, 138, 417–422. https://doi.org/10.1016/j.egypro.2017.10.188
310. Wenxin Shen, Wenzhe Tang, Atthaset Siripanan, Zhen Lei, Colin F. Duffield, David Wilson, Felix Kin Peng Hui & Yongping Wei .2017. Critical Success Factors in Thailand's Green Building Industry. Journal of Asian Architecture and Building Engineering, 16:2, 317-324. https://doi.org/10.3130/jaabe.16.317
311. National Housing Authority (NHA), Thailand. 2017. NHA's Affordable Housing in Thailand, a presentation by Krit Goenchanart (Director, Department of Housing Development Studies) Retrieved from https://datacenter.deqp.go.th/media/877970/10-11-2017-session-1-nhapresentation-bonn-germany.pdf
312. UNEP. 2018. Building for green growth in Thailand. Retrieved from https://www.unep.org/news-and-stories/story/building-green-growth-thailand
313. UNFCCC. NR-286 - Greening Thailand's Government Buildings. Retrieved from https://www4.unfccc.int/sites/PublicNAMA/_layouts/un/fccc/nama/NamaForRecognition.aspx?ID=199&viewOnly=1
314. IFC. 2020. IFC's Green Loan to Thailand's Top Hotel Group Will Help Drive Economic Recovery, Create Jobs. Retrieved from https://pressroom.ifc.org/all/pages/PressDetail.aspx?ID=25865
315. UNEP. 2019. Accelerating construction of energy efficient green housing units in Thailand (Project Identification Form). Retrieved from https://www.thegef.org/sites/default/files/web-documents/10189_CC_Thailand_PIF.pdf
316. CBI. 2020. ASEAN Sustainable Finance State of the Market Report 2020. Retrieved from https://www.climatebonds.net/files/reports/asean-sotm-2020.pdf
317. ADB. 2021. Summary of ADB Assistance to Thailand's National Housing Authority on Certification and Impacts of NHA's Green Housing Efforts (August 2021). Retrieved from https://www.nha.co.th/download/technical-report-on-adb-assistance-to-nha-on-green-housing/
318. UOB. 2021. UOB Thailand extends green loan to ACRE for eco-friendly residential development in Phuket. Retrieved from https://www.uobgroup.com/uobgroup/newsroom/2021/uob-thailand-extends-green-loan.page?path=data/uobgroup/2021/166&cr=segment
319. Ibid.
320. EEC Office. 2021. News Release. Retrieved from https://www.eeco.or.th/en/news/357
321. Ibid

322. Biospectrum Asia Edition. 2021. Thailand witnessed $1.7 billion investment in Bio-Circular-Green economic activities (BCG) during Jan-Sep 2020. Retrieved from https://www.biospectrumasia.com/news/102/17352/thailand-witnessed-1-7-billion-investment-in-bio-circular-green-economic-activities-bcg-during-jan-sep-2020.html
323. The ASEAN Secretariat. 2021. The Road to Sustainable Cities. The ASEAN. Issue 14: June-July 2021. Retrieved from https://asean.org/wp-content/uploads/2021/08/The-ASEAN-Sustainable-Cities-June-July-2021.pdf
324. Bangkok Post. 2021. 10 more areas picked to be developed into smart cities. Retrieved from https://www.bangkokpost.com/thailand/general/2188615/10-more-areas-picked-to-be-developed-into-smart-cities
325. The Nation. 2018. Experts contradict govt on coastal erosion. Retrieved from https://www.nationthailand.com/national/30339814
326. Japan International Cooperation Agency (JICA). 2010. The JICA Sector Study on Climate Change Program Loan in Thailand (Chapter 6 Coastal Erosion). Retrieved from https://openjicareport.jica.go.jp/pdf/12015442_03.pdf
327. Wanthongchai P., Pongruktham O. 2019. Mangrove Cover, Biodiversity, and Carbon Storage of Mangrove Forests in Thailand. In: Gul B., Böer B., Khan M., Clüsener-Godt M., Hameed A. (eds) Sabkha Ecosystems. Tasks for Vegetation Science, vol 49. Springer, Cham. https://doi.org/10.1007/978-3-030-04417-6_28
328. Oppenheimer, M., B.C. Glavovic , J. Hinkel, R. van de Wal, A.K. Magnan, A. Abd-Elgawad, R. Cai, M. Cifuentes-Jara, R.M. DeConto, T. Ghosh, J. Hay, F. Isla, B. Marzeion, B. Meyssignac, and Z. Sebesvari, 2019: Sea Level Rise and Implications for Low-Lying Islands, Coasts and Communities. In: IPCC Special Report on the Ocean and Cryosphere in a Changing Climate [H.-O. Pörtner, D.C. Roberts, V. Masson-Delmotte, P. Zhai, M. Tignor, E. Poloczanska, K. Mintenbeck, A. Alegría, M. Nicolai, A. Okem, J. Petzold, B. Rama, N.M. Weyer (eds.)]. In press. Retrieved from https://www.ipcc.ch/srocc/chapter/chapter-4-sea-level-rise-and-implications-for-low-lying-islands-coasts-and-communities/
329. https://openjicareport.jica.go.jp/pdf/12015442_03.pdf
330. World Bank and ADB. 2021. Climate Risk Country Profile: Thailand. Retrieved from https://reliefweb.int/sites/reliefweb.int/files/resources/climate-risk-country-profile-thailand.pdf
331. The Nature Conservancy. 2014. Mangroves for coastal defence. Retrieved from https://www.nature.org/media/oceansandcoasts/mangroves-for-coastal-defence.pdf
332. ONEP, MNRE. 2015. Thailand's Intended Nationally Determined Contribution (INDC). Retrieved from https://www4.unfccc.int/sites/ndcstaging/PublishedDocuments/Thailand%20First/Thailand_INDC.pdf
333. The Food and Agriculture Organization of the United Nations (FAO) and the International Union for Conservation of Nature and Natural Resources (IUCN). 2016. Mangrove-related policy and institutional frameworks in Pakistan, Thailand and Viet Nam. Retrieved from http://www.mangrovealliance.org/wp-content/uploads/2018/05/MFTF-Pakistan-thailand-vietnam.pdfm
334. Richards, D. R., & Friess, D. A. 2016. Rates and drivers of mangrove deforestation in Southeast Asia, 2000–2012. Proceedings of the National Academy of Sciences, 113(2), 344–349. https://doi.org/10.1073/pnas.1510272113
335. Kongkeaw, C., Kittitornkool, J., Vandergeest, P., & Kittiwatanawong, K. 2019. Explaining success in community based mangrove management: Four coastal communities along the Andaman Sea, Thailand. Ocean & Coastal Management, 178, 104822. https://doi.org/10.1016/j.ocecoaman.2019.104822
336. Spalding, Mark D and Leal, Maricé (editors). 2021. The State of the World's Mangroves 2021. Global Mangrove Alliance. Retrieved from https://www.mangrovealliance.org/wp-content/uploads/2021/07/The-State-of-the-Worlds-Mangroves-2021-FINAL-1.pdf
337. Earth Security. 2020. Financing the Earth's Assets: The Case for Mangroves as a Nature-based Climate Solution. Retrieved from https://earthsecurity.org/wp-content/uploads/2020/12/2128_ESG_mangrove_22.pdf
338. Spalding, Mark D and Leal, Maricé (editors). 2021. The State of the World's Mangroves 2021. Global Mangrove Alliance. Retrieved from https://www.mangrovealliance.org/wp-content/uploads/2021/07/The-State-of-the-Worlds-Mangroves-2021-FINAL-1.pdf
339. Flint, R., D. Herr, F. Vorhies and J. R. Smith 2018. Increasing success and effectiveness of mangrove conservation investments: A guide for project developers, donors and investors. IUCN, Geneva, Switzerland, and WWF Germany, Berlin, Germany. Retrieved from http://awsassets.panda.org/downloads/wwf_iucn_mangroves_investment_effectiveness_guide.pdf
340. Euromoney. 2018. Blue Finance: Why Marine PPPs could be a win-win-win. Retrieved from https://www.euromoney.com/article/b18hg7vjwmy9hn/blue-finance-why-marine-ppps-could-be-a-win-win-win
341. CBI. 2019. Latin America & Caribbean Green finance state of the market 2019. Retrieved from https://www.climatebonds.net/files/reports/cbi_lac_sotm_19_web_02.pdf
342. ADB. 2019. ADB Launches $5 Billion Healthy Oceans Action Plan. Retrieved from https://www.adb.org/news/adb-launches-5-billion-healthy-oceans-action-plan
343. Ibid.
344. FPO, BOT, SEC, OIC, and SET. 2021. Sustainable Finance Initiatives for Thailand. Retrieved from https://www.bot.or.th/Thai/SustainableBanking/Documents/Sustainable_Finance_Initiatives_for_Thailand.pdf
345. IEA. 2020. Putting a price on carbon – an efficient way for Thailand to meet its bold emission target. Retrieved from https://www.iea.org/articles/putting-a-price-on-carbon-an-efficient-way-for-thailand-to-meet-its-bold-emission-target
346. Business Inquirer. 2018. IFC issues Mabuhay bonds. Retrieved from https://business.inquirer.net/253026/ifc-issues-mabuhay-bonds
347. Power Technology. 2018. Philippines introduces new green bond worth $90m. Retrieved from https://www.power-technology.com/news/philippines-introduce-new-green-bond-worth-90m/
348. CBI. 2020. Thailand Sovereign. Retrieved from https://www.climatebonds.net/certification/Thailand-Sovereign
349. CBI. 2020. Thai Govt Marks 2020 with Certified Sovereign Green Issuance: Commitment to Recovery, Sustainability, Infrastructure. Retrieved from https://www.climatebonds.net/2020/12/thai-govt-marks-2020-certified-sovereign-green-issuance-commitment-recovery-sustainability
350. IFC. 2018. TMB Issues Thailand's First Green Bond for $60 Million. Retrieved from https://pressroom.ifc.org/all/pages/PressDetail.aspx?ID=18347
351. CBI. Green Bond Factsheet (TMB). Retrieved from https://www.climatebonds.net/files/files/2018-06%20TH%20TMB%20Bank.pdf
352. Bangkok Post. 2021. Toyota Leasing issues B2bn green debenture. Retrieved from https://www.bangkokpost.com/business/2122315/toyota-leasing-issues-b2bn-green-debenture
353. ThaiBMA. Bond information. Retrieved from https://www.thaibma.or.th/EN/BondInfo/BondFeature/Issue.aspx?symbol=TLT235B
354. ADB. 2019. ADB Invests 3 Billion Thai Baht in Energy Absolute's Green Bond for Wind Farm Development. Retrieved from https://www.adb.org/news/adb-invests-3-billion-thai-baht-energy-absolutes-green-bond-wind-farm-development
355. CBI. Energy Absolute. Retrieved from https://www.climatebonds.net/certification/energy-absolute
356. IFC. 2018. TMB Issues Thailand's First Green Bond for $60 Million. Retrieved from https://pressroom.ifc.org/all/pages/PressDetail.aspx?ID=18347
357. ADB. 2018. Thailand Green Bond Project: Report and Recommendation of the President. Retrieved from https://www.adb.org/projects/documents/tha-52292-001-rrp
358. UOB. 2021. UOB Thailand extends green loan to ACRE for eco-friendly residential development in Phuket. Retrieved from https://www.uobgroup.com/uobgroup/newsroom/2021/uob-thailand-extends-green-loan.page?path=data/uobgroup/2021/166&cr=segment
359. DB. 2020. Report and Recommendation of the President to the Board of Directors: Proposed Loan Energy Absolute Public Company Limited Green Loan for Renewable Energy and Electric Vehicle Charging Network (Thailand). Retrieved from https://www.adb.org/sites/default/files/project-documents/54268/54268-001-rrp-en.pdf
360. David, Sören (Head of the Technical Support Unit, NAMA Facility). 2017. Financing NAMA Activities – how to prepare a "bankable" NAMA Proposal, a presentation to the Anglophone African Regional Workshop on "Finance ready mitigation actions: building blocks for NDC achievement", 25-27 April, Accra, Ghana. Retrieved from https://www.nama-facility.org/fileadmin/user_upload/events/workshop_finance_ready_mitigation_actions_accra_ghana_NAMA_facility_presentation.pdf
361. Halstead, Matthew and Xander van Tilburg. 2015. NAMA Financial Component: A Portfolio Guarantee Scheme (PGS), a presentation at the ECN/TGP-EEDP workshop, June 25 2015. Retrieved from https://thai-german-cooperation.info/userfiles/4_Financial%20components%20of%20NAMA.pdf
362. GIZ Thailand. Thailand Refrigeration and Air Conditioning Nationally Appropriate Mitigation Action (RAC NAMA). Retrieved from http://www.nama-facility.org/fileadmin/user_upload/NAMA_Facility_NSP_Document_ThaiRAC.pdf
363. Thai ESCO Association. 2014. Thai ESCO Association & ESCO Business Model", a presentation to Inter-regional Workshop on Energy Efficiency Investment Projects Pipeline. 23-24 April, 2014. Bangkok, Thailand. Retrieved from https://unece.org/fileadmin/DAM/energy/se/pp/gee21/Worshop_Bangkok_April_14/Session_7d_Vejakit.pdf
364. Hee Kong Yong. 2017. Infrastructure Financing in Malaysia. Nomura Journal Of Asian Capital Markets. Spring 2017 Vol.1/No.2 Retrieved from https://www.nomurafoundation.or.jp/wordpress/wp-content/uploads/2017/04/NJACM1-1SP17-06.pdf
365. OECD and ASEAN. 2021. ASEAN Risk Mitigation Instruments Database (RMID): Thailand. Retrieved from https://rmid-oecd.asean.org/database/public-interventions/public-interventions-of-asean-member-states/thailand/
366. ADB. 2021. Green Yellow Rooftop Solar Project: FAST Report. Retrieved from https://www.adb.org/projects/documents/tha-53283-001-rrp
367. DFDL. 2021. Thailand Legal Update: Green Building Energy Standards. Retrieved from https://www.dfdl.com/uncategorized/thailand-legal-update-green-building-energy-standards/
368. Ibid.
369. Department of Alternative Energy Development and Efficiency (DEDE), MOE. Future of Energy Efficiency in Thailand, a presentation by Wisaruth Maethasith (Bureau of Energy Regulation and Conservation) Retrieved from https://iea.blob.core.windows.net/assets/imports/events/613/TheFutureofEnergyEfficiencyinThailandWisaruthMaethasith.pdf
370. Thai Green Building Institute (TGBI). 2017. Thai's Rating of Energy and Environmental Sustainability for Existing Building: Operation and Maintenance (TREES – EB Version 1.0). Retrieved from https://tgbi.or.th/uploads/trees/2017_03_TREES-EB-Eng.pdf
371. TGBI. 2017. Thai's Rating of Energy and Environmental Sustainability for New Construction and Major Renovation (TREES –NC Version 1.1) Retrieved from https://www.tgbi.or.th/uploads/trees/2017_03_TREES-NC-Eng.pdf
372. TGBI. 2017. Thai's Rating of Energy and Environmental Sustainability for Preparation of New Building Construction & Major Renovation (TREES PRE NC Version 1.1) Retrieved from https://www.tgbi.or.th/uploads/trees/2017_03_TREES-PreNC-Eng.pdf
373. TGBI. 2017. Thai's Rating of Energy and Environmental Sustainability for New Construction and Major Renovation and Core and Shell Building (TREES -NC /CS). Retrieved from http://lgc.tgbi.or.th/uploads/trees/2017_03_TREES-CS-Eng.pdf
374. Lohmeng, A., Sudasna, K., & Tondee, T. 2017. State of The Art of Green Building Standards and Certification System Development in Thailand. Energy Procedia, 138, 417–422. https://doi.org/10.1016/j.egypro.2017.10.188
375. TGBI website. Database on projects that passed assessment. Retrieved from https://tgbi.or.th/directory/project-2/
376. ASEAN Centre for Energy (ACE) and GIZ. 2018. Mapping of Green Building Codes and Building Energy Efficiency in ASEAN: Towards Guidelines on ASEAN Green Building Codes. Retrieved from https://aseanenergy.sharepoint.com/PublicationLibrary/Forms/AllItems.aspx?id=%2FPublicationLibrary%2F2018%2FACE%20Publications%2FAGEP%20%2D%20Report%20on%20Mapping%20Green%20Building%20Codes%20in%20ASEAN%2C%202018%2Epdf&parent=%2FPublicationLibrary%2F2018%2FACE%20Publications&p=true
377. Chutarat, Acharawan. 2013. Building Labels and Certification in Thailand. Retrieved from http://www.thai-german-cooperation.info/download/20131029_10_pdp_building_labels_certification.pdf
378. TEI. 2011. "A Guide to The Thai Green Label Scheme (Fifth Edition June 2011). Retrieved from https://data.thailand.opendevelopmentmekong.net/en/dataset/a-guide-to-thai-green-label-scheme/resource/23a540c1-78e2-472a-bba8-62c29f3e5f50/proxy#:~:text=The%20Green%20Label%20is%20an,foods%2C%20beverage%2C%20and%20pharmaceuticals
379. Pairoj-Boriboon, Sirithan. 2014. Green Labeling Scheme and Green Public Procurement in Thailand, a presentation to "International Symposium on Green Public Procurement and Ecolabeling toward Sustainable Consumption and Production in ASEAN Region", 11th – 12th December 2014, Tokyo. Retrieved from https://www.env.go.jp/policy/hozen/green/kokusai_platform/2014symposium/05Thailand.pdf
380. TEI. 2021. Green Label Products Certification July 2021. Retrieved from http://www.tei.or.th/greenlabel/en/download/2021-07-Name-GL-eng.pdf
381. ADB. 2021. Summary of ADB Assistance to Thailand's National Housing Authority on Certification and Impacts of NHA's Green Housing Efforts (August 2021). Retrieved from https://www.nha.co.th/download/technical-report-on-adb-assistance-to-nha-on-green-housing/
382. ACMF. 2018. ASEAN Green Bond Standards. Retrieved from https://www.sc.com.my/api/documentms/download.ashx?id=75136194-3ce3-43a2-b562-3952b04b93f4
383. Ibid.
384. Conventuslaw. 2019. Sustainable Financing in The ASEAN Region. Retrieved from http://www.conventuslaw.com/report/sustainable-financing-in-the-asean-region/
385. ACMF. 2018. ASEAN Sustainability Bond Standards. Retrieved from https://www.sc.com.my/api/documentms/download.ashx?id=3c4f768f-a290-4722-b9d1-ef55942fbfde
386. Globalethicalbanking. 2018. ASEAN Launches Social and Sustainability Bond Standards. Retrieved from https://www.globalethicalbanking.com/asean-launches-social-sustainability-bond-standards/
387. Vietnam Certification Centre (QUACERT). ISO 14001. Retrieved from http://www.quacert.gov.vn/en/iso-14001.iso254.html
388. Intarajinda, R., Sriamonkitkul, W., Chutiprapat, V., Bhasaputra, P., & Pattaraprakorn, W. 2011. The Successive Implement of ISO 9001, ISO 14001 & OHSAS 18001 for Large Enterprises in Thailand. Greater Mekong Sub-Region Academic and Research Network (GMSARN), 225-230. Retrieved from http://gmsarnjournal.com/home/wp-content/uploads/2015/08/vol5no4-4.pdf
389. Vietnam Certification Centre (QUACERT). ISO 50001. Retrieved from http://www.quacert.gov.vn/en/iso-50001-energy-management-system-enms.iso259.html
390. Intarajinda, R., Sriamonkitkul, W., Chutiprapat, V., Bhasaputra, P., & Pattaraprakorn, W. 2011. The Successive Implement of ISO 9001, ISO 14001 & OHSAS 18001 for Large Enterprises in Thailand. Greater Mekong Sub-Region Academic and Research Network (GMSARN), 225-230. Retrieved from http://gmsarnjournal.com/home/wp-content/uploads/2015/08/vol5no4-4.pdf
391. ADB 2018. Promoting Green Local Currency Bonds for Infrastructure Development in ASEAN+3. Retrieved from https://www.adb.org/sites/default/files/publication/410326/green-lcy-bonds-infrastructure-development-asean3.pdf
392. CBI's database
393. U.S. Green Building Council (USGBC). 2021. What is LEED? Retrieved from https://www.usgbc.org/help/what-leed
394. MRTA. Chiang Mai Mass Transit Project (Red Line). Retrieved from https://www.mrta.co.th/en/projectelectrictrain/regional-major-cities/chiangmai/?AspxAutoDetectCookieSupport=1#head4
395. MRTA. Nakhon Ratchasima Mass Transit Project (Green Line). Retrieved from https://www.mrta.co.th/en/projectelectrictrain/regional-major-cities/nakhonratchasima/